Charleston Entertains

SEASON by SEASON

Charleston Entertains

SEASON by SEASON

BY
Ann Copenhaver Cotton
Henrietta Freeman Gaillard
Jo Anne Joyner Willis, R.D.

PHOTOGRAPHS BY
N. Jane Iseley

HISTORICAL SKETCHES BY
Thomas Savage, Jr.

ART DIRECTION BY
Alice Turner Michalak

LEGACY PUBLICATIONS
A Subsidiary of Pace Communications, Inc.
Greensboro, North Carolina

ISBN 0–933101–15–5

Library of Congress
Catalog Card Number: 91–62822

Designed by Richard Stinely

Edited by Debra J. Bost

Borders by Louis Luedtke

We are grateful to the University of South Carolina Press for permission to quote from the following book, hereafter cited as "Charleston, S.C., in 1774 as Described by an English Traveller":

H. Roy Merrins, editor. *The Colonial South Carolina Scene, Contemporary Views, 1697–1774* (Columbia: University of South Carolina Press, 1977), 280–289. "Charleston, S.C., in 1774 as Described by an English Traveller," originally published in *Historical Magazine*, IX (November 1865), 341–347.

Printed in the United States of America

This book is dedicated to our mothers:

Mary Glenn Stone Copenhaver
Emmie Tompkins Freeman
Nancy Vincent Iseley
Fannie Ann Florine Thacker Joyner
Jean Nauman Savage
Virginia Lewis Turner

Acknowledgments

The authors wish to express their deep appreciation to the following:

Evan and Buddy Atkins, Agnes L. Baldwin, Sallie Barnes, Suzanne P. Barnwell, Norma Beerman, Chuck Beringer, Glover Beringer, Janice S. Bigger, Yvonne Bishop, Rosie Blessing, Brother Boniface, Barbsie and Nelson Brown, David Brown, Darlene Brumfield, Mr. and Mrs. Frank Brumley and Robert Burbage.

Dr. and Mrs. J. Price Cameron, Jr., Heyward Carter, Vicki T. Chambers, The Charleston Museum, Nancy Willis Clayman, Anne Cleveland, Eliza Cleveland, Richard Coen, Vereen Coen, Marsha Childs Copenhaver, Mary Glenn S. Copenhaver, Ben Cotton, Jay Cotton, Magdalyn D. Cotton, Phil Cotton, Pat Cutter, Annie Dalton, Alberta Dixon, Susan Davis, Judy Doering, Ralph Doering and Virginia K. Donehue.

Drayton Hall, a property of the National Trust for Historic Preservation, Larry Duckworth, Gov. and Mrs. James B. Edwards, Kathy Ellett, Koiner Ellett, Anna Lee Willis Eppright, Charlotte Fairey, Happy Faust, Nancy Fisher, Mr. and Mrs. Darryl Forrester and Emmie T. Freeman.

Emmie Gaillard, John Gaillard, Lucy Gaillard, Palmer Gaillard, Susan Gaillard, *Gateway Magazine*, Lillian Goldberg, Ginny Good, Sarah Graham, Judy Joyner Griffin, Sheila L. Hammer, Harris Teeter Foods, Betsy Harvey, Mammie Hartwell, Historic Charleston Foundation, Gedney M. Howe III and Mrs. Thomas A. Huguenin.

Juanita Johnson, Florine Thacker Joyner, Dottie Kerrison, Kathryn King, Mary Stone Klingelhofer, Mr. and Mrs. W. Jefferson Leath, Mr. and Mrs. Austin Letson, Sarah Lindsay, Magnolia Plantation and Gardens, Manigault House, Helen Maybank, Eliza McDowell, Mr. and Mrs. Joseph H. McGee, The Middleton Place Foundation and Sara Ellen Munnerlyn.

Teenie Parks, Gail Paul, Claudia Phillipps, George and Melou Piegari, Harold Pratt-Thomas, Lou Ann Pratt-Thomas, Mr. and Mrs. Henry L. B. Ravenel, Red Food Stores of Chattanooga, Edmund Rhett, Sally Rhett, Bob and Mary Dean Richards, Kitty Robinson and Roper Hospital Foundation.

Dot Saab, Helen Scarborough, Sher Silver, Sallie Sinkler, Anne F. Smith, Nancy Smith, Cam Stuhr, Jane Stelling, Margaret V. Stone, Mary Lu Stone and Winnie Stone.

Anna Troxler, Rhett Thurman, Boo Townsend, Helen Warren, Frankie H. Webb, Mrs. Ben Scott Whaley, Anne Elliott J. Willis, E. B. Harrison Willis, Eddie Willis, Helen Burns Willis, Dr. and Mrs. G. Fraser Wilson, Lula Wilson, Carolyn and De Worrell, Jonell Worrell, Lillian Yarborough, Rita L. Yarborough and Mr. and Mrs. Joseph R. Young.

Contents

Introduction

I AM NOT ORIGINALLY from Charleston. My palate was developed on delicacies from the Chesapeake on the Eastern Shore of Virginia where my father's family has lived for generations. Neither am I known for any prowess in the kitchen, my few attempts at cooking having ended in miserable failure. Why then, you may ask, am I contributing to this book? The simple answer is that it does not take a master chef to appreciate Charleston's superb culinary reputation. And as a historian, I am struck by the extraordinary continuum in dining traditions that survives here. Charlestonians have been eating shrimp and hominy at breakfast for generations — who can blame them? New World staples have rarely come together to produce such a satisfying meal.

The diversity of the people of early Charleston contributes significantly to the varied local diet. In many households, recipes, or "receipts" as they are still called here, have been handed down for generations, collected perhaps, as George Rogers writes in *Charleston in the Age of the Pinckneys,* "from a French grandmother or a Santo Domingan grandmother or a German passing through Charleston or a lady from England — or brought home after diplomatic assignments in Europe." The melding of these different cultures makes it possible to detect strains of French, English, Irish, African and West Indian heritage in local dishes.

As a port city, Charleston had access to imported delicacies from around the world. The Duke of Saxe-Weimar, visiting Charleston in 1826, was delighted to find in the city market "the most beautiful tropical fruit therein arranged, oranges from Florida, pistachios, and large excellent pine apples from Cuba." Imported wines were particularly valued. Dr. George Milligen-Johnston observed in 1770, "Madeira Wine and Punch are the common Drinks of the Inhabitants; yet, few Gentlemen are without Claret, Port, Lisbon, and other Wines, of the French, Spanish or Portugal Vintages. The Ladies, I mention it to their credit, are extremely temperate, and generally drink water." Some found the Charleston gentleman's love of wine and spirits excessive. The Reverend Alexander Garden, an eighteenth-century rector of St. Philip's Church, had disdain for "the gentlemen planters, who are absolutely above every occupation but eating, drinking, lolling, smoking, and sleeping, which five modes constitute the essence of their life and existence."

The times for meals in early Charleston varied from household to household. Breakfast was often a substantial morning repast of hominy, leftover cold meat, bacon, eggs, cold shrimp and tomatoes. By the eighteenth century, dinner at three o'clock in the afternoon was the norm. This hour was dictated by the plantation work day and tropical climate and allowed a full morning of labor. Immortalized in Josephine Pinckney's *Three O'Clock Dinner*, it is a ritual still observed by many Charleston families. Supper was usually a light meal except on those evenings when a lavish entertainment such as a ball was given. The prescribed hour for ball suppers was eleven o'clock.

We have a firsthand glimpse of the meals enjoyed by Carolinians through the remarkable survival of several early receipt books prepared by South Carolina ladies. Sarah Rutledge, the daughter of Edward Rutledge, a signer of the Declaration of Independence, published a large collection of recipes gathered from friends in 1847. Titled *The Carolina Housewife, or House and Home*, it is still available today in facsimile editions. Almost a century before, in 1756, Eliza Lucas Pinckney had prepared a small collection of recipes and cures for illnesses. Twenty-six of these appeared again in the receipt book kept by her daughter Harriott Pinckney Horry, the mistress of Hampton Plantation. Instructions such as "To dress a calves head in imitation of Turtle" and "To Ragout a Breast of Veal" suggest the complicated nature of food preparation in a preindustrial society.

One of the most amazing references to an elaborate main course is found in the nineteenth-century diary of John Grimball. He records a dinner for eight in Charleston that included a "preserve of fowl, this consisted of a dove stuffed into a quail, the quail into a guinea hen, the hen into a duck, the duck into a capon, the capon into a goose, and that in turn into a peacock or turkey and so roasted and cut into transverse sections." Obviously, visitors who tasted these local delights never forgot them.

The menus presented here are our attempt to present a picture of the way Charlestonians entertain today. Photographed in some of the city's most important museum properties and private houses, there are recipes whose origins are deeply rooted in the Lowcountry's culinary history. Others represent more modern tastes and later cooking developments. Charleston cookery has been applauded by gourmets both ancient and modern. We invite you to share in this rich heritage.

TOM SAVAGE

New Year's Day Buffet
The Judge Robert Pringle House

CHARLESTON'S culinary year begins with New Year's Day. Whether humble or grand, no Lowcountry New Year's celebration is complete without collard greens and Hoppin' John, a distinctly local combination of rice, cow peas, and salt pork or ham. According to tradition, the former guarantees prosperity in the new year, the latter good luck.

Rice has meant good luck in South Carolina since the early eighteenth century. Introduced in the 1690's, Carolina rice offered the perfect link to the British mercantile system and was eminently suitable for the vast stretch of flat, tidal lowlands that extend fifty miles from the sea. This is the Carolina Lowcountry, linked to its urban center, Charleston, by inland waterways and to European markets by the Atlantic Ocean. "At Charleston, the Ashley and Cooper rivers meet to form the Atlantic Ocean," goes an old saying. There was more than a little truth to this for the planters and merchants who grew rich from the cultivation and export of rice, the "Carolina gold" of the Colonial period.

Charlestonians have remained faithful to rice, giving some credence to the old saying that compares Charleston residents to the Chinese: They both speak in a foreign dialect, live behind walls, worship their ancestors and eat rice with every meal. While today's staple is more likely grown in Texas, commercial cultivation in Carolina having

The border above is taken from a Drayton Hall overmantel detail.

ceased earlier this century, rice dishes in their seemingly infinite variety remain an important link to Charleston's prosperous past.

When Judge Robert Pringle completed his Tradd Street mansion in 1774, Charleston was at its zenith, the fourth-largest city in Colonial America after Philadelphia, New York and Boston, and the South's only urban center. Robert Pringle had immigrated from Scotland to Charleston as a young man in 1725, joining other Scots who made up a sizeable sector of Charleston's pre-Revolutionary commercial community. His success as a merchant and judge is reflected in the fine single house he built on land deeded in trust by his father-in-law, prominent merchant Andrew Allen.

The single house is Charleston's unique contribution to American architectural history. With the narrow gable end facing the street, the plan is well suited to the city's original long and narrow lots. Only one room in width and two in depth, divided by a bisecting passage, the single house also provided some comfort during hot and humid summers by allowing cross ventilation. In the eighteenth century, piazzas were usually confined to one story. In the nineteenth century, however, they often rose for three or even four stories, providing scenic outdoor living spaces on all floors.

Pringle's pride in his new town residence is evidenced by the stone marker with his initials and the date, 1774, which he placed by the door on the upper piazza. The house served his descendants until 1886. The family of the present owners has lived here since 1909.

From the first-floor piazza, one enters the house across a mahogany threshold using the massive cypress door with its original lock and key. Once inside, today's visitor encounters spacious rooms with their original Georgian woodwork of cypress, a handsome backdrop for the accumulated treasures of generations.

THE interior parts of South Carolina are very well water'd by numbers of fine fresh water rivers abounding with different kind of good fish, such as trout, perch, and plenty of craw fish. The soil mends as you go 15 or 20 miles inland from Charles Town where instead of sand you then begin to meet with different sorts of clay, loom [sic], or good rich black earth, most of which is in general very fertile and will produce almost anything that is sown upon it in great abundance, particularly rice and indigo, which are the staples of this province and are both very profitable to the planters. . . .

"Charleston, S.C., in 1774 as Described by an English Traveller"

NEW YEAR'S DAY BUFFET

Serves 12 to 16

Bloody Marys
Pickled Shrimp
Fresh Ham • Hoppin' John
Harold's Collard Greens
Baked Apples • Baked Onions
Orange and Avocado Salad
Corn Bread
Pepper Relish
Baked Custard
Old-Fashioned Molasses Cookies

Bloody Marys

Yields 16 to 18 6-ounce servings

2 46-ounce cans tomato juice
1 pint vodka
4 tablespoons Worcestershire sauce
6 tablespoons lemon juice
1 teaspoon salt
⅛ teaspoon pepper
¼ teaspoon Tabasco
Dash of celery salt

Pour all the ingredients into a 1-gallon jug. Shake well and refrigerate several hours. Serve with celery stalks or dill pickle spears, if desired.

• Pickled Shrimp

Yields 16 servings

2 tablespoons salad oil
1 pint tarragon vinegar
¾ teaspoon salt
¾ teaspoon pickling spice
1½ teaspoons celery seed
Few drops of Tabasco
½ teaspoon dry mustard
3 medium Bermuda onions, sliced
6 bay leaves
2½ pounds shrimp, cooked and peeled

Combine the salad oil, vinegar and spices. Mix well. Layer the shrimp, onions and bay leaves in a 2-quart container. Pour the salad oil mixture over the shrimp. Chill at least 24 hours; will keep a week.

Orange and Avocado Salad

Yields 12 servings

2 11-ounce cans mandarin oranges,
    drained; or 1½ cups fresh orange sections
1 6-ounce can sliced black olives, drained
1 cup Italian dressing
2 avocados, peeled and sliced
1 13¾-ounce can artichoke hearts,
    drained and coarsely chopped
4 to 5 cups salad greens of your choice,
    washed and drained

In a large bowl, combine orange sections and olives with Italian dressing; marinate overnight. When ready to serve, add sliced avocados and artichoke hearts to marinade. Add salad greens and toss gently to coat. Serve immediately.

· Fresh Ham

Yields 12 or more servings

1 12-pound fresh ham or pork loin
1 cup water
1 cup vinegar
1 tablespoon salt
1 tablespoon seasoned black pepper
2 tablespoons butter
1 teaspoon red pepper
1 teaspoon prepared mustard

Remove skin from fresh ham and place in roasting pan, fat side up. Place on bottom rack in oven at 250°. Combine the remaining ingredients and baste frequently, at least every 30 minutes. Cook covered; remove cover for the last hour. Ham should be well done; cook at least 30 minutes per pound, or until the meat thermometer reaches 170°. Pour any remaining sauce on ham before serving.

· Hoppin' John
Yields 6 to 8 servings

½ pound dried cow peas or black-eyed
  peas, rinsed
1 quart water
1 small onion, chopped
2 stalks celery, chopped
6 slices bacon, cooked and crumbled
1 cup raw rice, rinsed
Salt and pepper to taste

Soak the peas overnight in water. Remove the peas that float to the top. Drain. In a 2½-quart saucepan, cover peas with one quart water. Season with salt and pepper. Simmer uncovered one hour or until peas are tender. (Be sure to check the water level frequently.) Remove from heat and drain, saving the liquid. Place rice in the top of rice steamer; cover the rice with the pea liquid, adding water if necessary. Add onions and celery. Steam rice for about 25 minutes. Flake rice with a fork; add the peas and crumbled bacon and steam until rice is cooked, about 30 minutes. (Note: This recipe does not double well; it is better to make two recipes to serve 12 to 16 people.)

· Harold's Collard Greens
Yields 12 servings

3 pounds collard greens
3 tablespoons sugar
6 tablespoons bacon fat
Salt and pepper to taste

Wash and clean greens; tear off stems. Place greens, sugar and bacon fat in Dutch oven; fill almost to the top with water. Cook over low heat for 1½ to 2 hours. Drain. Season with salt and pepper and serve.

· Baked Apples
Yields 8 servings

8 apples
Juice of ½ lemon
4 tablespoons butter, cut into pieces
½ cup brown sugar
½ cup raisins
¾ cup Amaretto or apple juice

Preheat oven to 375°. Wash apples and core to within ½ inch of the bottom. Peel top half of apples. Blend together butter and brown sugar; stir in raisins. Fill the apples with raisin mixture. Place apples in a 9-by-12-inch baking dish. Pour Amaretto over apples. Bake for 50 to 60 minutes, until tender but not mushy.

• Baked Onions
Yields 10 to 12 servings

6 medium Bermuda onions, sliced
¾ cup (1½ sticks) butter, divided
1 recipe of White Sauce
Salt and pepper to taste
¾ pound sliced Swiss cheese
1 loaf small-diameter French bread, sliced
¼ to ½ inch thick (enough to cover the
top of casserole)

In a saucepan over medium heat, sauté onions in 1 stick of butter. Place onions in a greased 13-by-9-inch dish; cover with White Sauce. Season. Arrange cheese on top. Spread remaining butter on French bread. Arrange slices of bread, butter side up, on top of onions. Bake at 350° for 30 minutes or until golden brown and bubbly.

WHITE SAUCE
Yields 1½ cups

3 tablespoons butter
3 tablespoons flour
1 cup milk
½ cup chicken broth
½ teaspoon salt
¼ teaspoon white pepper

In a 2-quart saucepan, melt butter on medium heat. Add flour to butter and blend thoroughly. Using a wire whisk, slowly add milk and chicken broth. Cook until thickened. Add seasonings. Remove from heat and set aside.

• Corn Bread
Yields 18 squares

2 cups corn meal
2 cups flour
2 cups milk
6 eggs
1 cup (2 sticks) butter, melted

Mix corn meal, flour, milk, butter and eggs in a bowl. Pour into 2 greased 8-inch-square ovenproof dishes. Bake at 400° for 25 minutes or until golden brown. This recipe may be halved.

Pepper Relish
Yields 8 pints

12 red bell peppers
12 green bell peppers
12 hot peppers
12 medium onions
¼ cup salt
1 quart vinegar
3 cups sugar

Remove seeds from peppers and grind together with onions. (Be sure to use gloves to seed the hot peppers.) Mix salt with pepper mixture. Put in a cloth bag and let drip overnight. In a saucepan, mix vinegar with 3 cups of sugar; bring to a boil. Empty pepper mixture into a large pot; pour vinegar mixture over the pepper mixture and bring to a boil again. Boil for 20 minutes. Put in sterilized pint jars, seal, and process. Pepper relish should be made in the late summer. Before serving, 1 teaspoon hot pepper sauce and 2 teaspoons Worcestershire sauce may be added to each pint, if desired.

◆ Baked Custard

Yields 12 servings

2½ cups milk
¾ cup sugar
6 eggs
1½ teaspoons vanilla
Pinch of salt
Ground nutmeg, optional

Preheat oven to 300°. In a pan large enough to hold 12 custard cups, pour ½ inch hot water; place in oven. Beat together milk and sugar until foamy. Add eggs, vanilla and salt and beat for 2 minutes. Pour into individual custard cups and place in pan. Sprinkle with nutmeg, if desired. Bake 40 minutes until set, and brown around the edges, and knife inserted in the center comes out clean.

◆ Old-Fashioned Molasses Cookies

Yields 48 cookies

1 cup (2 sticks) plus 2 tablespoons butter
1¼ cups sugar, divided
¼ cup molasses
1 egg
2½ cups flour
2 teaspoons baking soda
1 teaspoon cinnamon
1 teaspoon ground ginger
¼ teaspoon ground cloves

Preheat oven to 350°. Grease baking sheets. Cream butter, 1 cup sugar, molasses and egg in large bowl using electric mixer. Mix flour, baking soda, cinnamon, ginger and cloves in medium bowl. Add to butter mixture and mix until dough forms. Roll dough into walnut-size pieces; drop balls into a bowl containing remaining sugar. Roll balls in sugar and place on baking sheets; press flat with spatula. Bake until crisp and golden, about 10 to 12 minutes. Especially good served warm.

FACING PAGE

A nineteenth-century Meissen compote is filled with flowers amid heirloom silver for a New Year's Day celebration in the dining room of the Judge Robert Pringle house.

*Under an impressive
nineteenth-century chandelier,
a sumptuous cocktail buffet
awaits guests before the ball.*

*Egg, Avocado and
Caviar Mold displayed
alongside Crudité Tray
and Dipping Sauce.*

*Beef Tenderloin served
on a nineteenth-century
Chinese export platter.*

Cocktails Before the Ball
The William Pinckney Shingler House

WHEN SUCCESSFUL Charleston businessman and cotton factor William Pinckney Shingler purchased this property from the Limehouse family in 1856, it was one of the largest residential tracts in the city. The magnificent late–Greek Revival mansion he built was one of the last great Charleston houses constructed before the Civil War. Shingler's signature appears on the Ordinance of Secession signed in Charleston on December 20, 1860, and he would later serve as a colonel in the Confederate cavalry.

The spacious and inviting dining room at the back of the house is entered after passing through double drawing rooms with rich plaster cornices and rococo-revival marble mantels. A Federal carved wood mantel graces the dining room, its original marble predecessor having shattered during Charleston's devastating earthquake of 1886. At night, the sparkling nineteenth-century crystal chandelier casts a warm glow over family silver and Chinese export porcelain, making this a sumptuous and romantic setting for cocktails before the ball.

Balls have been an important element in Charleston's social season since the eighteenth century and visitors rarely failed to be impressed. Visiting New Englander Josiah Quincy attended the St. Cecilia assembly in 1773 and found the company impressively dressed.

In loftiness of head-dress these ladies stoop to the daughters of the north, in richness of dress surpass them. The gentlemen many of them dressed with richness and elegance uncommon with us — many with swords on. We had two Macaronis present — just arrived from London. This character I found real, and not fictitious. 'See the Macaroni' was common phrase in the hall.

Now confined to several of Charleston's spacious public buildings, balls in the nineteenth century more often than not were given in the private houses large enough to accommodate the limited society of the day. Margaret Manigault attended one of Mrs. Thomas Radcliffe's celebrated balls in 1809 and wrote to Alice Izard,

General Wilkinson's band charmed us with some well executed military pieces — during which we paced up and down the spacious corridor which was brilliantly illuminated, and into her handsome bed room, which was likewise lighted. A variety of cake, and wine, and fruit, and jellies, and all the nice things that could be collected were handed about. Everybody was in high spirits — they danced, and the band played during the intervals of dining — at eleven o'clock some delicious little oyster patties were brought up with other things of the same kind — after which the gentlemen were invited to partake of a supper of beefstakes and cold turkies. . . . The party did not break up until two o'clock.

Given the spaciousness of Charleston's grander nineteenth-century dwellings with their expansive drawing rooms, dining rooms and impressive halls, these festive occasions saw their reception rooms put to good use.

COCKTAILS BEFORE THE BALL

Serves 50 to 60

Beef Tenderloin
Glazed Smithfield Ham
Mayonnaise • Spicy Mustard • Jezebel Sauce
Crudité Tray and Dipping Sauce
Egg, Avocado and Caviar Mold
Tortellini with Dipping Sauces
Claudia's Shrimp in Chafing Dish
Oysters on the Half Shell
Mushroom Pinwheels
Pralines • Scottish Shortbread

Beef Tenderloin

Yields 60 generous servings

3 4- to 6-pound tenderloins
Worcestershire sauce
Seasoned black pepper
Garlic salt
Flour

Preheat oven to 450°. Remove fat from roasts. Spear all over with fork. Sprinkle with pepper and garlic salt; rub into meat. Pour Worcestershire over tenderloins; using a sifter, dust meat with flour. Place in 450° oven for 20 minutes; reduce temperature to 350° and cook 20 to 30 minutes longer. Slice and serve with assorted breads; especially good with thinly sliced whole wheat and rye.

To decorate as in picture, mix 1 package unflavored gelatin with ⅓ cup cold water until dissolved, then add ⅓ cup hot water; mixture should be of pourable, thin consistency. Using pastry brush, apply a thin layer of gelatin mixture to cooled tenderloins. Decorate top of one-third to one-half of one tenderloin with flower design of your choice. Apply another coat of gelatin mixture; refrigerate until ready to serve. Use decorated portion as centerpiece for tray.

Glazed Smithfield Ham

Yields 100 servings

1 12- to14-pound cured Smithfield ham
Whole cloves
¼ cup brown sugar
2 tablespoons white sugar

Using a vegetable brush, thoroughly wash ham in warm water. Soak overnight in cold water. Fill a ham boiler or large pot with enough water to cover ham and place on stove. When water begins to boil, place ham in pot with skin side up. Place lid on pot. Reduce heat and simmer ham about 20 to 25 minutes per pound or until tender. Remove ham from pot. Before ham cools, remove skin. Place ham in baking pan, fat side up. Diagonally score fat using diamond or square designs. Place a whole clove in each square. Mix brown and white sugar together and rub into ham fat Bake in a 300° oven until brown, 20 to 30 minutes. Cool and refrigerate before slicing. Serve with party-size rolls.

Mayonnaise

Yields 1½ pints

2 eggs, room temperature
1 heaping teaspoon mustard
4 to 5 dashes of Tabasco
1 teaspoon salt
1 24-ounce bottle salad oil
1 teaspoon vinegar or lemon juice

Place eggs in mixing bowl, food processor or blender with salt, mustard and Tabasco. Beat together, gradually adding oil. Beat briefly after mixed. Add vinegar or lemon juice and beat a few seconds longer.

Spicy Mustard

Yields 4 cups

1 cup dry mustard
1 cup white vinegar

3 eggs
1 cup sugar

Soak mustard in vinegar overnight. Beat eggs until light and fluffy. Add sugar and continue to beat. Add mustard and vinegar, mixing well. Cook in top of double boiler 15 minutes, stirring constantly. Remove, pour into container and refrigerate.

Jezebel Sauce

Yields 2½ cups

1 18-ounce jar pineapple preserves
1 18-ounce jar apple jelly
1 small can of dry mustard
   (approximately 1 ounce)
1 5-ounce jar prepared horseradish
1 tablespoon freshly ground pepper

Combine all ingredients and blend well. Keeps indefinitely in the refrigerator. Serve with pork, roast beef or venison. Also delicious over cream cheese.

Crudité Tray
and Dipping Sauce

Even in the winter, there is a colorful variety of fresh vegetables available for a crunchy, low-calorie addition to party fare. The usual offering of carrots, celery, broccoli and cauliflower can be enhanced by many exotic vegetables from a good produce department. Here is a combination with some variety that will be avail-

able at most grocers. Amounts and selections can be adjusted to your taste.

3 pounds green beans
1 pound snow peas
2 to 3 Belgian endive
4 purple-topped turnips
2 pounds small mushrooms
4 red bell peppers

Beans. Leave beans whole but check carefully and remove stems. Bring 6 quarts water to a rapid boil. Drop in beans and allow them to boil for 4 to 5 minutes. Drain. Immediately plunge beans into ice water to stop the cooking and preserve the bright green color. Spread beans on towel-lined racks to dry. Refrigerate until time to serve. Leftovers are delicious sautéed with butter or stir-fried with any other vegetables.

Snow Peas. Remove stems and strings and follow above procedure but stop cooking after 1 minute.

Endive. Separate heads of endive into leaves. Wash carefully in cold water. Allow to dry and refrigerate.

Turnips. Peel and slice. Cut into strips.

Mushrooms. Clean with damp brush or soft cloth. Cut away woody part of stem and leave whole. These store best in a cloth bag in the refrigerator.

Bell Peppers. Remove stalk and seeds. Slice peppers into strips. Refrigerate.

Arrange vegetables with attention to color and texture. Dip is attractive when served in hollowed-out vegetables such as bell pepper, eggplant, or purple cabbage.

Continued . . .

DIPPING SAUCE FOR VEGETABLES
  Yields 4 cups

2 8-ounce packages cream cheese, softened
1½ cups mayonnaise
½ cup ketchup
1 onion, grated
2 teaspoons Worcestershire sauce
4 teaspoons French dressing

Blend all ingredients together and refrigerate overnight.

Egg, Avocado and Caviar Mold
Yields 40 servings

2 envelopes of gelatin
½ cup water

Soften gelatin in cold water; dissolve over low heat. Two tablespoons of this will be used for each layer, so reheating may be necessary.

EGG LAYER

8 hard-boiled eggs, mashed
1 small onion, finely chopped
2 tablespoons mayonnaise
2 tablespoons dissolved gelatin

Blend ingredients in a food processor and place in a greased 9-inch springform pan. This will be the first layer. Put pan in refrigerator while preparing the next layer.

AVOCADO LAYER

2 avocados, peeled and sliced
½ cup sour cream
1 tablespoon mayonnaise
4 tablespoons chopped green onion
2 tablespoons dissolved gelatin

Blend ingredients in a food processor and spread on top of the egg layer in the springform pan.

TOPPING

1 8-ounce package cream cheese, softened
1 8-ounce container sour cream
2 tablespoons dissolved gelatin
4 ounces black or red caviar, washed and thoroughly drained
Chopped parsley

Blend the cream cheese, sour cream and dissolved gelatin together. Place on top of the avocado layer. Chill overnight. When ready to serve, remove sides from the springform pan. Decorate top with caviar and around the bottom with chopped parsley. To decorate as in picture, cut your own design in wax paper. Carefully pat caviar dry; gingerly spoon over top to cover design. When ready to serve, lift wax paper. Serve with crackers.

Tortellini with Dipping Sauces
Yields 40 servings

2 teaspoons salt
4 quarts water
4 pounds tortellini, green and white
2 teaspoons olive oil

In a large kettle, bring salt and water to a rolling boil. Add tortellini, cooking just until tender. Remove from heat; drain the pasta. Place pasta in a large bowl; add olive oil to prevent sticking.

Skewer tortellini on fancy toothpicks; arrange on platter. Serve with Dipping Sauces on page 19.

CRÈME FRAÎCHE
  Yields 2 cups

2 cups heavy cream
3 tablespoons buttermilk

In a glass bowl, mix the cream and buttermilk together. Let stand at room temperature 10 to 12 hours, or until mixture is thick.

GARLIC SAUCE
  Yields 2 cups

2 cups Crème Fraîche
2 garlic cloves, crushed
1½ tablespoons Worcestershire sauce

Mix ingredients together; refrigerate until ready to serve.

LEMON DILL SAUCE
  Yields 2 cups

2 cups Crème Fraîche
⅓ cup freshly grated Parmesan cheese
¼ cup fresh lemon juice
1 to 2 garlic clove, crushed
1 teaspoon dried dill weed

Mix ingredients together. Chill overnight.

Claudia's Shrimp in Chafing Dish

Yields 25 servings

3 8-ounce packages cream cheese, softened
¾ cup (1½ sticks) butter, softened
2 bunches green onions, chopped
9 cups shrimp, cooked, peeled, deveined and chopped

Blend together cream cheese and butter.

Add onion and shrimp. Chill overnight. Right before serving time, heat on high in microwave until soft, about five minutes. Transfer to a chafing dish and garnish with parsley and whole peeled, cooked shrimp. Serve with crackers.

Oysters on the Half Shell

Serves 50

150 oysters, in half shells

To make opening oysters easier, put oysters in 400° oven for 5 to 7 minutes. Then drop them into ice water. Arrange oysters on a bed of crushed ice. Serve with lemon wedges, Sour Cream Dip, or Cocktail Sauce (see page 168).

SOUR CREAM DIP
  Yields 2 cups

2 cups sour cream
2 tablespoons horseradish
1 teaspoon salt
½ teaspoon paprika
Dash of Tabasco
1 eggplant or red cabbage, hollowed out

Mix together the sour cream, horseradish, salt, paprika and Tabasco. Put in small dish that will fit into the eggplant and serve.

Mushroom Pinwheels

Yields 40

8 ounces fresh Shitake mushrooms, chopped
8 ounces fresh button mushrooms, chopped
6 green onions, sliced
3 tablespoons butter
3 tablespoons dry white wine

Continued . . .

2 tablespoons diced pimento
2 tablespoons snipped parsley
¼ teaspoon sage, crushed
¼ teaspoon pepper
⅛ teaspoon thyme, crushed
1 egg yolk
6 sheets phyllo dough, thawed, halved into
    12-by-9-inch sheets, covered with damp
    cloth
¼ cup butter, melted and divided
2 tablespoons fine, dry bread crumbs

Sauté mushrooms and onions in 3 table-spoons of butter. Add wine and cook for several minutes. Remove from heat and stir in pimento, parsley, sage, pepper and thyme. Cool for 10 minutes. Place half of mixture in food processor and add egg yolk; mix. Combine the mushroom mix-ture from the food processor with the rest of the mushrooms.

Layer six of the halved phyllo sheets on one large, ungreased baking sheet, brush-ing melted butter on each. Sprinkle half of the bread crumbs down the length of one side of the phyllo within 3 inches from long edge and 1½ inches of the short side.

Spoon half of the mushroom mixture over the bread crumbs. Fold short edges of phyllo toward center; roll jelly-roll style from long side nearest filling. Brush roll with melted butter. Cut diagonal slits 1 inch apart but not through mushroom mixture. Using another baking sheet, repeat to make second roll.

Bake in 400° oven 15 to 18 minutes or until golden brown. Cool 5 minutes. Cut into slices. These should be passed.

Pralines
Yields 50 small pralines

1½ cups pecans
1½ cups sugar
¾ cup light brown sugar, packed
½ cup milk
⅜ cup (¾ stick) of butter
1 teaspoon vanilla

Roast pecans at 275° for 20 to 25 min-utes. Combine all ingredients in a heavy saucepan and bring to a boil. Cook to the soft ball stage (238° to 240°), stirring constantly. Remove from heat and add vanilla. Stir until mixture thickens and becomes creamy and cloudy. Using a tea-spoon, spoon onto buttered waxed paper. Allow to cool and store in tin.

Scottish Shortbread
Yields 25 to 30 squares

1 pound (4 sticks) butter, softened
1½ cups sugar
6 cups flour

Cream butter and sugar. Add flour, one cup at a time. Press dough into ungreased 11-by-15-inch pan. Use cookie stamp to imprint dough if desired. Bake at 325° for 25 to 35 minutes. Cut into squares while hot. Let cool in pan. Store in tight-ly covered tin; do not freeze. Note: This recipe works best when made with real butter.

Dessert After Dock Street
The James Huston House

CHARLESTON'S Dock Street Theatre opened February 12, 1736, with a performance of George Farquhar's *The Recruiting Officer*. It was an auspicious beginning for what would develop as Charleston's passion for the theatre, culminating in the season of 1773–74 when 118 performances, including eleven of Shakespeare's plays, were given for the enjoyment of Charleston audiences.

The original Dock Street Theatre having been destroyed in the eighteenth century, Alexander Calder purchased the property in 1809 and moved his celebrated Planters Hotel to a house at the corner of Queen and Church streets. It flourished and expanded, but by the 1930's had become a near ruin. Under President Roosevelt's WPA program, the facade and lobby of the old Planters Hotel were used in a reconstruction of the old Dock Street Theatre which reopened in 1937 with a performance of, appropriately, *The Recruiting Officer*.

In the reconstruction of the theatre, the magnificent Federal-period decorative plaster and woodwork from the demolished Thomas Radcliffe mansion of 1805 were installed to form a handsome reception room. It has been witness to many festive occasions, including a sumptuous Race Week ball in 1809, recorded by Margaret Manigault:

> Hers [Mrs. Radcliffe's] was a complete Ball — for it concluded with a magnificent supper at which near eighty persons were seated. The

centre of it was adorned with an accumulation of iced plumb cakes in a kind of bower of natural flowers which gave the whole a very gay appearance — the table was loaded with every dainty that could be thought of, every precaution was taken for the accommodation of so large a party. We slipped away immediately after, at about one o'clock, and got home safe.

When the dessert course concluded an elaborate seated dinner, it was customary to remove the tablecloth and serve dessert on the bare wooden surface of the dining table. Visiting Bostonian Josiah Quincy dined with Thomas Smith of Broad Street in 1773 and enjoyed a ". . . decent and plenteous table of meats; the upper cloth removed, a compleat table of puddings, pies, tarts, custards, sweetmeats, oranges, macarones, etc., etc., — profuse. Excellent wines." Quincy also dined at Miles Brewton's impressive town mansion and recorded, "A most elegant table, three courses, nick-nacks, jellies, preserves, sweetmeats, etc. After dinner, two sorts of nuts, almonds, raisins, three sorts of wines, apples, oranges, etc. By odds the richest wine I ever tasted."

Dessert courses are perhaps a bit less lavish today in concept but not less enjoyable in content. Our post–Dock Street party is presented in the library of the house built adjacent to the Planters Hotel by prosperous merchant tailor James Huston in 1809. Only the large windows and door facing Church Street suggest the room's original, humbler function as a tailor's shop. It is now a beautifully restored private residence, and its owners frequently welcome visiting performers and audiences to enjoy the hospitality of modern Charleston within its walls. Mrs. Radcliffe would approve.

DESSERT AFTER DOCK STREET

Serves 24

Crepes Suzette
Trifle
Chocolate Toffee Meringue Torte
White Chocolate Cheesecake
with Mocha-Dipped Strawberries
Lemon Charlotte with Apricot Sauce
Bourbon Pecan Tart
Spiced Pecans
Naked Pilgrims
Amaretto Coffee • Irish Coffee

Crepes Suzette
Yields sauce for 24 crepes

1 recipe Dessert Crepes
1 orange
½ cup orange juice
½ cup (1 stick) butter
1 tablespoon sugar
½ cup Curaçao or Cointreau or Triple Sec
½ cup Grand Marnier

Using a sharp paring knife, peel thinnest layer of peel from orange. Cut into very narrow strips enough peel to suit taste—at least 1 tablespoon. In crepe pan or chafing dish, melt butter. Stir in orange juice, sugar and Curaçao or other liqueur. Fold crepes into quarters and place in sauce, turning and spooning sauce to coat. When all crepes have been added to pan, pour Grand Marnier gently over all. Heat without stirring. Ignite with match. (When Crepes Suzette is the only dessert, allow three per person.)

DESSERT CREPES
Yields 24 crepes

4 eggs
1 cup flour
2 tablespoons oil
½ teaspoon salt
2 teaspoons sugar
1 cup milk

Beat eggs well; add other ingredients, beating until smooth. Lightly grease small skillet; heat until a drop of water dances on bottom. Pour in 2 to 3 tablespoons batter and cook until lightly browned on both sides. Remove and stack crepes with wax paper between. Crepes may be refrigerated or frozen at this stage.

Trifle
Yields 20 to 24 servings

1 package yellow cake mix
2 eggs
1⅓ cups water
2 recipes Boiled Custard (see page 189)
2 cups fresh or frozen unsweetened blueberries
2 cups fresh or frozen unsweetened strawberries, sliced
2 cups fresh or frozen unsweetened peaches, peeled and sliced
1½ cups plus 2 tablespoons sugar
16 ounces strawberry preserves
1 cup whipping cream
Chocolate curls, optional
Toasted almonds, optional
Whole strawberries, optional

CAKE

Make yellow cake mix according to package directions, but using 2 eggs and 1⅓ cups water. (A sponge cake recipe may be substituted.) Bake in 4 9-inch layer pans for 25 minutes or until cake tests done using a cake tester. Cool layers.

FRUIT

Sprinkle ½ cup sugar on each type of fruit and set aside.

First Layer. In a 9-inch trifle bowl, place

one layer of cake. Spread ½ cup strawberry preserves to the edge of the bowl, sealing the cake. Top with a layer of 2 cups of one type of fruit. Cover fruit with 1 cup Boiled Custard.

Second Layer. Place another layer of cake on top of the custard. It may be necessary to use some of the fourth layer of cake to make the cake meet the sides of the trifle bowl. Repeat layering of preserves, 2 cups fruit and 1 cup custard.

Third Layer. Repeat second layer. Beat whipping cream until stiff peaks form, adding 2 tablespoons sugar. Spread whipped cream over third layer, sealing to side of bowl. Garnish with chocolate curls, almonds, or strawberries if desired.

This may be made ahead and refrigerated up to 24 hours.

Chocolate Toffee Meringue Torte
Yields 8 to 10 servings

MERINGUE

5 egg whites, room temperature
Pinch of cream of tartar
¾ cup sugar
1¾ cups powdered sugar
⅓ cup cocoa

Using an inverted 8-inch round or square cake pan, trace 3 circles or squares on waxed paper and cut out. Place a small dab of solid shortening on bottom of each circle (to anchor on baking sheet) and place on baking sheets; set aside. Beat egg whites and cream of tartar in a large bowl until egg whites hold soft peaks. Beat in sugar, 2 tablespoons at a time, beating until egg whites hold stiff peaks. Sift powdered sugar with cocoa and fold into egg whites. Divide meringue equally among waxed paper circles or squares, spreading evenly to the edges. Bake 45 minutes to 1 hour at 300° or until meringues are firm in the center. (Baking sheets may need to be rearranged during baking time.) When baked, remove meringues to wire racks to cool. Layers can be made 2 to 3 days in advance and stored in an airtight container.

TOFFEE CREAM FILLING

6 1.1-ounce English toffee–flavored candy bars
2 cups whipping cream, whipped
Chocolate curls or 2 1.1-ounce English toffee–flavored candy bars, crushed

Freeze candy bars. Place candy bars in thick plastic bag and crush finely with a hammer. Gently fold crushed candy into whipped cream. Spread whipped-cream between layers as they are stacked; frost top and sides of meringue layers. Cover loosely and chill 8 hours or up to 24 hours. Garnish with chocolate curls or additional crushed candy before serving, if desired. For ease in slicing, dip sharp knife in hot water between each slice.

White Chocolate Cheesecake with Mocha-Dipped Strawberries
Yields 12 to 14 slices

CRUST

1 8½-ounce package chocolate wafers
3 tablespoons sugar
¼ cup pecans
5 tablespoons butter, melted

Put the wafers, sugar, and pecans in food processor. Process until finely crushed. Butter a 9-inch springform pan. Press wafer crust into the bottom and up the sides of the prepared pan. Chill while Filling is made.

FILLING

½ cup (1 stick) butter, room temperature
2 pounds cream cheese, room temperature
4 eggs
1 pound white chocolate, melted
1 tablespoon vanilla extract

In a large bowl, beat the cream cheese until light and fluffy. Add eggs, one at a time. Beat in softened butter and melted white chocolate. Add vanilla extract. Carefully spoon into chocolate crumb crust. Bake at 300° for 1½ hours. Cool completely. Cover and refrigerate until cold. Garnish with Mocha-Dipped Strawberries.

MOCHA-DIPPED STRAWBERRIES

1 ounce semisweet chocolate, coarsely chopped
1½ teaspoons brewed coffee
1 teaspoon coffee liqueur
10 to 15 beautiful strawberries with stems

In double boiler, melt chocolate with coffee and liqueur. Stir until smooth. Dip bottom half of strawberry in chocolate. Arrange with stems up on waxed paper. Refrigerate until chocolate is set.

Lemon Charlotte with Apricot Sauce
Yields 8 to 10 servings

7 egg yolks
1¼ cups sugar
½ cup lemon juice
2 teaspoons lemon zest or grated lemon rind
1 package unflavored gelatin
¼ cup cold water
7 egg whites
½ pint whipping cream, whipped
1 package plain ladyfingers, split
Apricot Sauce, optional

In double boiler, beat egg yolks with sugar until lemon colored. Add juice and rind. Cook over boiling water until thickened, whisking with a wire whip. Remove from heat. Soften gelatin in cold water; add to hot mixture, stirring until dissolved. Beat egg whites until stiff; fold into hot mixture. Fold in whipped cream. Line a 2-quart springform pan with ladyfingers. Spoon lemon mixture over ladyfingers. Chill several hours until set, then unmold. Cut into wedges. Serve with Apricot Sauce, if desired.

APRICOT SAUCE
  Yields ¾ cup

¼ cup apricot preserves
2 tablespoons orange marmalade

2 tablespoons orange juice
1 tablespoon lemon juice
2 tablespoons butter
⅓ cup slivered almonds

In medium saucepan, over low heat, melt together preserves, marmalade, orange juice and lemon juice. Add butter and almonds. Bring to a boil. Remove from heat. Serve at room temperature. Top each serving of Lemon Charlotte with a spoonful of sauce.

Bourbon Pecan Tart
Yields 6 to 8 servings

1 recipe Cream Cheese Pastry
  (see Mincemeat Pie, page 190)
2 eggs
1 cup dark corn syrup
½ cup firmly packed brown sugar
1 tablespoon melted butter
2 tablespoons bourbon
1 teaspoon vanilla extract
1 to 1¼ cups chopped pecans

Roll out dough for Cream Cheese Pastry ¼-inch thick on a floured surface. Fit into a 10-inch round tart pan with a removable fluted rim; chill for 30 minutes. Line the shell with wax paper and fill with raw rice; bake at 425° for 15 minutes or until pale golden. Carefully remove the rice and paper.

In a bowl, combine the eggs, corn syrup and brown sugar; beat until thoroughly blended. Stir in butter, bourbon, vanilla and pecans. Carefully spoon filling into shell. Bake at 350° for 20 to 25 minutes or until the center is firm. Cool, remove rim of pan; slide tart onto a platter and serve.

Spiced Pecans
Yields 2 cups

2 tablespoons butter, margarine or oil
2 cups pecan halves
½ cup sugar
½ to 1 teaspoon salt
½ teaspoon chili powder
⅛ teaspoon crushed red pepper flakes, optional

In an iron skillet, heat the butter over low to medium heat. Add the pecan halves; sauté until the pecans become golden brown, or about 15 minutes. Remove the pecans from the heat; toss in a bowl with sugar, salt, chili powder and red pepper flakes. Serve warm or at room temperature. Store in an airtight container.

Naked Pilgrims
Yields 6 servings

1½ pints French Vanilla ice cream
½ cup Kahlua
½ cup Amaretto
Milk to fill blender container
¼ cup slivered almonds, toasted

In a blender, combine the above ingredients except for the almonds. Serve in long-stemmed glasses and sprinkle with almonds.

Amaretto Coffee

Yields 6 servings

¼ cup ground coffee
1 teaspoon vanilla extract
1 teaspoon almond extract

Sprinkle extracts over ground coffee and brew as usual. May double recipe. Dollop with whipped cream, if desired.

Irish Coffee

Yields 1 serving

6 ounces hot brewed coffee
1 jigger Irish whiskey
1 to 2 teaspoons sugar
Whipped cream

In a coffee cup, stir together coffee, whiskey and sugar. Add a dollop of whipped cream on the top.

FACING PAGE

Ancestral portraits preside over dessert in the terra-cotta library of the James Huston house. Irish Coffee and Amaretto Coffee accompany Spiced Pecans, White Chocolate Cheesecake with Mocha-Dipped Strawberries, Trifle and Chocolate Toffee Meringue Torte.

A plantation Easter dinner is celebrated in the spacious dining room of Halidon Hill.

Endive Salad with Shrimp and
Mrs. Scarborough's Rémoulade Sauce.

A Meringue Basket with Strawberries and Sugar
Shapes add a seasonal touch to Easter dinner.

Plantation Easter
Halidon Hill Plantation

STRETCHING north from Charleston, the Cooper River system is particularly rich in surviving early plantation houses and Anglican churches. One of the most interesting among the latter is Pompion Hill Chapel, a "Chapel of Ease" for the north riding of St. Thomas Parish. Built between 1763 and 1765, the chapel was used in conjunction with the parish church and held monthly services for the convenience or "ease" of the residents of the northern section of the parish. Its intriguing name "Pompion" means, and is pronounced locally, "pumpkin." Incised in bricks on the sides of both doors are the initials of the builders Zachariah Villepontoux, a brickmaker and builder, and William Axson, the brick mason for the job. Arched windows, a projecting chancel with Venetian window, and slate-covered jerkinhead roof add architectural sophistication to the building which has been called "a miniature Georgian masterpiece."

Repaired in 1825, having been "in decay" for years, the building was restored again in 1843 and in 1855. After the Civil War it was used only infrequently, but in recent years, descendants of parishioners have come to the rescue and cared for this fascinating reminder of early Anglicanism in the Lowcountry.

Nearby is Halidon Hill Plantation, another lucky recipient of rescue efforts. In 1954, it was moved four miles through woods and beautifully restored on a site originally part of Middleburg, the plantation of French Huguenot Benjamin Simons. Halidon Hill house was originally known as Quinby, named for Quenby Hall, the English

The border above is from window surrounds in the James Huston house.

estate of the Ashby family who received the land by grant in 1681. The original house at Quinby was destroyed at the time of the American Revolution. In 1792 the property was advertised for sale: "Quinby Plantation for sale, about 26 miles from Charleston containing 158 acres of rice land in the very best pitch of tide. 1,045 acres of high land contiguous to several fine springs of water."

The buyer was Roger Pinckney, who is credited with the building of the present frame house shortly after his purchase of the property. Inside, the interiors exhibit the sophisticated Federal decoration more often associated with town mansions. The dining room is wainscoted with a chair rail decorated with gouge work and marbleized baseboards. A handsome mantel with applied neoclassical plasterwork is symmetrically placed at one end of the room which is crowned with a dentil cornice. Among the handsome furnishings is a unique Charleston-made inlaid china press in the Federal style, its glazed upper and lower doors revealing early silver and Spode-Copeland china.

Easter dinner is a festive occasion for family members. Spring flowers from the garden arranged in a tureen and white lace placemats adorn the highly polished pedestal table in the spacious dining room, ready for Easter afternoon guests.

PLANTATION EASTER

Serves 12

Easter Sunrise
Piroshki with Piquant Herb Dip
Deviled Eggs
Roast Leg of Lamb • Crème de Menthe Jelly
Rosemary Potatoes
Fresh Asparagus with Tangy Lemon Sauce
Endive Salad with Shrimp
Mrs. Scarborough's Rémoulade Sauce
Brioches • Raspberry/Blueberry Chutney
Meringue Basket with Strawberries
Sugar Shapes • Chocolate Truffles

Easter Sunrise

Yields 12 servings

2 6-ounce cans frozen pineapple juice
   concentrate
2 6-ounce cans frozen orange juice
   concentrate
3 cups water
½ teaspoon Angostura bitters
2 10-ounce bottles sparkling water
12 ounces vodka

Combine pineapple juice, orange juice, water and bitters; stir until juices thaw. May refrigerate at this stage. At serving time add sparkling water and vodka. Garnish with fresh pineapple spears and orange slices if desired, and serve in tall glasses over ice.

Piroshki

Yields 30 triangles

½ pound finely ground beef or veal
½ cup minced onions
½ cup (1 stick) butter, melted, divided
2 hard-cooked eggs, chopped
1 teaspoon chopped capers
1 teaspoon chopped chives
1 teaspoon chopped parsley
1 teaspoon sour cream
Salt and pepper to taste
12 Phyllo pastry leaves, well covered
   and defrosted

Sauté meat and onion in 1 to 2 teaspoons melted butter. Add eggs, capers, chives, parsley and sour cream and heat thor-oughly. Season to taste with salt and pepper. Set aside.

Uncover pastry and remove one leaf; brush well with butter and cover with second leaf, brushing with butter again. Cover unused pastry with damp towel. Cut the buttered phyllo into five strips along the short edge. Place a teaspoon of filling about one inch from the top of the first strip. Fold a top corner across and continue to fold diagonally as if folding a flag. Tuck in any excess dough. Place triangle on greased baking sheet and brush lightly with butter. Repeat steps until all filling is used. Triangles may be refrigerated for several hours before baking or they may be frozen for baking later. Bake at 400° for 20 minutes or until golden brown. Serve with Piquant Herb Dip.

Piquant Herb Dip

Yields 2½ cups

½ cup dry white wine
½ cup parsley sprigs
¼ cup white vinegar
1 small onion, quartered
2 cloves garlic
2 teaspoon dried tarragon
¼ teaspoon dried chervil
⅛ teaspoon pepper
1 cup mayonnaise

Place first eight ingredients in blender and blend until uniformly chopped. Pour mixture into saucepan and cook over medium heat until reduced to ⅓ cup. Strain. Return liquid to pan and stir in mayonnaise. Garnish with parsley.

Deviled Eggs

Yields 12 servings

6 hard-cooked eggs
2 tablespoons mayonnaise
2 tablespoons sour cream
Pinch of salt
1½ teaspoons Dijon mustard
Dash of cayenne pepper
3 tablespoons chopped, salted almonds,
   toasted

Cut eggs in half lengthwise and scoop out yolks. In a small bowl, mash yolks with mayonnaise and sour cream; add salt and mustard and blend well. Taste for seasoning; add more to taste. Add a dash of cayenne pepper. Refill egg whites with yolk mixture and sprinkle with chopped almonds.

Roast Leg of Lamb

Yields 12 servings

1 7-pound leg of lamb
1 garlic clove, slivered
Salt
Freshly ground pepper
3 tablespoons Dijon mustard
¼ cup brown sugar
1 cup strong coffee
1 cup Burgundy

Preheat oven to 400°. Make small slits in lamb. Insert garlic slivers and season generously with salt and pepper. Spread with mustard. Sprinkle with brown sugar. Combine coffee and wine. Place lamb, uncovered, in roasting pan; baste with wine mixture. Reduce temperature to 350°. Roast 30 minutes per pound for well done or until meat thermometer registers 175° to 180°, basting periodically. Serve with Crème de Menthe Jelly or mint jelly.

Crème de Menthe Jelly

Yields 4 8-ounce jars

2½ cups sugar
1 cup water
1 6-ounce can frozen lemonade concentrate
1 package liquid fruit pectin
½ cup Crème de Menthe

Bring sugar and water to a boil, stirring constantly; boil hard for 1 minute. Remove from heat. Stir in lemonade, pectin and Crème de Menthe. Mix well. Skim quickly and pour into sterilized 8-ounce jars. Seal.

Rosemary Potatoes

Yields 8 servings

3 pounds tiny new potatoes, scrubbed
Branches of rosemary, 3 inches long, enough
   for number of potatoes
2 tablespoons butter, melted
⅛ teaspoon salt
¼ teaspoon freshly ground pepper

Preheat oven to 400°. In a 4-quart saucepan, cover potatoes with water. Cook over high heat until potatoes are partially cooked. Drain and cool slightly. Remove most of the leaves from the center of the rosemary branches, leaving a cluster of leaves at either end. Starting at the thicker end, skewer the potatoes onto the branches, being sure to stop when bare part of branch is inside potato. Place the potatoes on a baking sheet and drizzle with the butter; roll the branches to distribute the butter evenly. Season with the salt and pepper and bake until the potato skins are golden brown and crisp, about 25 minutes.

Fresh Asparagus with Tangy Lemon Sauce
Yields 12 servings

3 to 3½ pounds fresh asparagus
2 eggs
⅔ cup (1⅓ sticks) butter
2 teaspoons sugar
1 teaspoon cornstarch
½ cup lemon juice
2 teaspoons grated lemon rind

Bend asparagus until the tough end snaps off. Cook in boiling water, salted if desired, until crisp-tender, about five minutes, depending on the thickness of stalks. Meanwhile, beat the eggs in the top container of a double boiler. Bring water in the bottom to a boil. To the eggs, add butter, sugar and cornstarch. Cook until butter melts and mixture begins to thicken. Add lemon juice and

continue to cook until thickened again. Drain asparagus and gently remove to platter. Pour lemon sauce over asparagus and sprinkle with lemon rind.

Endive Salad with Shrimp
Yields 12 servings

1 head curly endive, washed and drained
2 heads Belgian endive, washed and drained
60 large shrimp, peeled, deveined and cooked

Line 12 salad plates with curly endive. Place 2 leaves of Belgian endive on each plate. Arrange 5 large shrimp in a circle in center of greens. Serve with Mrs. Scarborough's Rémoulade Sauce or your favorite salad dressing.

Mrs. Scarborough's Rémoulade Sauce
Yields 2½ cups

¼ cup tarragon vinegar
¼ cup mustard
¼ cup lemon juice
¼ cup horseradish
2 teaspoons salt
1 tablespoon paprika
Dash black pepper
Dash hot pepper
2 tablespoons ketchup
2 teaspoons sugar
¾ cup salad oil

½ cup minced green onions including tops
½ cup minced celery

Combine the first 10 ingredients in a blender; blend until smooth. Gradually add oil and blend again. Stir in onion and celery but do not blend these. This keeps well in the refrigerator. Delicious with seafood or as a salad dressing.

Brioches
Yields 2 large or 24 small brioches

1 cup milk
½ cup (1 stick) butter
3 tablespoons plus 1 teaspoon sugar
1 package dry yeast
2 teaspoons salt
2 eggs
4 to 4½ cups flour
1 tablespoon vegetable oil
1 egg white

Combine milk, butter and 3 tablespoons sugar in a large saucepan and heat until butter is melted. Cool to lukewarm (105° to 115° degrees). When cool, stir in yeast and let stand for 10 minutes. Stir in salt. Add eggs, beating well. Stir in 2 cups of flour, mix well using electric mixer. Stir in remaining flour by hand. Knead on a floured surface until dough is elastic and tacky—about 10 minutes. Pour vegetable oil over dough, coating ball of dough well. Cover and allow to rise until doubled in bulk—about 2 hours. Punch dough down. Allow to rest 5 minutes.

For two large brioches, use brioche pans 6 inches in diameter and 3½ inches high; for small brioches, use muffin tins with cups 1½ to 2 inches in diameter. Grease pans or muffin cups. Form a large ball of dough to fit pans or tins; moisten finger slightly and make a depression in each large ball; place a small ball of dough in each depression—approximately 1½ inches in diameter for large brioches, ½ inch in diameter for small brioches. Cover and let rise until doubled in bulk —approximately 1 hour.

For a shiny glaze, beat 1 egg white with 1 teaspoon sugar; brush over brioches. For large brioches, bake at at 375° for 30 to 40 minutes or until golden brown; for small brioches, bake at 375° for 15 to 20 minutes. Loaves will sound hollow when thumped. Cool slightly before unmolding.

Raspberry / Blueberry Chutney
Yields 4 cups

½ cup white vinegar
¼ cup water
¼ cup currants
¼ cup golden raisins
½ teaspoon crushed red pepper flakes
2 tablespoons olive oil
2 medium onions, minced
1 teaspoon minced garlic
¼ cup sugar
1½ pounds green tomatoes, unpeeled, chopped
1 tablespoon lemon juice

Continued . . .

1 cup blueberries
1 cup raspberries

In a small saucepan, combine the vinegar with water and bring to a boil over high heat. Add currants, raisins and hot pepper. Reduce heat and simmer for 1 minute. Remove from heat and set aside.

In a large skillet, heat the olive oil. Sauté onions over moderate heat, stirring occasionally, until softened and translucent—about 5 minutes. Add garlic, cover and cook 2 minutes longer. Add the sugar and increase the heat to high. Stir in the reserved currants, raisins, hot pepper and liquid, bring to a boil, stirring, until the liquid thickens, 2 to 3 minutes. Add the tomatoes, cover and cook over medium heat, stirring frequently, until very tender, 5 to 7 minutes. Stir in lemon juice and remove from the heat. Let cool for 10 minutes.

Fold in the blueberries and raspberries and let cool to room temperature. Cover tightly and refrigerate for up to 3 days before serving. Remove from the refrigerator 30 minutes before serving time.

Meringue Basket with Strawberries

Yields 1 4-by-6-inch basket

3 egg whites at room
 temperature
1 teaspoon vanilla
1 teaspoon white vinegar
1 teaspoon water
Pinch salt

1 cup sugar
2 quarts fresh strawberries, capped
½ pint whipping cream, whipped

Beat egg whites until peaks form. Add vanilla, vinegar, water and salt and continue beating. Add sugar gradually, 1 tablespoon at a time until mixture is very stiff and holds shape well. Bake on well-greased wax paper on cookie sheet for 3 to 4 hours at 200°. Continue baking until they are completely dry and hollow-sounding. Use for Easter basket or any desired shape. This recipe makes enough meringue for 12 individual shells, or three 8-inch layers for a torte.

To make a basket: Spread a 4-by-6-inch rectangle of meringue ¾ inch thick for basket bottom. On the same cookie sheet, make a frame about 1 inch wide and 1 inch high, the same 4-by-6-inch dimensions. On another prepared cookie sheet, make two more identical frames, and a u-shaped tube for the handle. Save ¼ cup of meringue to use as "glue." Bake at 200° for 3 to 4 hours.

To assemble: Dot small amount of the leftover meringue around outside edge of base. Stack first frame in place to create sides for basket. Repeat with remaining two frames. Since meringues are so fragile, handle works best just propped in place once the basket is filled with fruit or ice cream. Bake entire basket another 1 to 2 hours at 200°. Remove to large serving platter.

To serve: Fill basket to overflowing with strawberries. Use any remaining berries to garnish platter. Slice to serve, scooping extra berries from platter. Dollop each serving with whipped cream.

Sugar Shapes
Yields 6 to 7 dozen cookies

3 cups flour
2 teaspoons cream of tartar
1 teaspoon baking soda
½ teaspoon salt
1 cup (2 sticks) margarine or butter
2 eggs
1 cup sugar
1 teaspoon vanilla

Mix dry ingredients together in medium mixing bowl. Cut in margarine or butter and blend completely. This may be done in a food processor. Beat eggs and add sugar and vanilla. Add egg mixture to flour mixture and blend well. Divide dough into thirds, wrap in plastic or wax paper and chill for at least 1 hour. This may be done several days ahead. Preheat oven to 350°. Sprinkle pastry cloth with flour or a mixture of flour and powdered sugar; working with one-third of the dough at a time, roll out to ⅛ inch thickness. Cut into desired shapes. Transfer to lightly oiled cookie sheets and bake for 10 minutes until lightly browned. Remove from cookie sheets while still hot. These may be decorated with colored sugar before baking, or with icing after baking.

Chocolate Truffles
Yields 16 truffles

⅓ cup heavy cream
2 tablespoons Kahlua
6 ounces semisweet chocolate, melted
¼ cup (½ stick) butter, room temperature
Powdered cocoa

In a heavy saucepan, boil cream until reduced to 3 tablespoons. Remove from heat, stir in Kahlua. Add melted chocolate and butter. Using a wire whisk, stir until mixture is smooth. Pour into shallow bowl and refrigerate. Using a melon baller or teaspoon, scoop into 1½-inch balls. Roll in powdered cocoa or chocolate sprinkles. Put in foil candy cups. Store in refrigerator until ready to use.

If using candy mold, spray mold of desired shape with vegetable baking spray. Pour melted chocolate mixture into mold, reserving small amount for putting candy together. Refrigerate for 1 hour or more—mixture must be very firm. Remove each ball of candy from mold and spread a small amount of melted chocolate on each half. Press halves together and refrigerate until ready to use.

Garden Luncheon
The James Verree House

OF CHARLESTON'S many historic and picturesque streets, Church Street is perhaps the most alluring. As its name suggests, several of the city's historic houses of worship are located here. At the head of the street is St. Philip's Church with its magnificent steeple, housing Charleston's oldest Anglican congregation. Just down the street from St. Philip's is architect E. B. White's 1845 French Huguenot Church, one of the city's first essays in pure gothic revival and a reminder of early Charleston's sizeable French Protestant population. Below Tradd Street is Robert Mills' First Baptist Church, built between 1819 and 1822 for the descendants of the early Anabaptist refugees from Kittery, Maine, who came to Carolina in 1683. Of his own creation Mills wrote, "The Baptist Church of Charleston exhibits the best specimen of taste in architecture in the city. It is purely Greek in its style, simply grand in its proportions, and beautiful in its detail."

Interspersed among these ecclesiastical structures is a rich collection of domestic architecture from the eighteenth and nineteenth centuries. Grand "double houses," Charleston's ubiquitous "single houses," and several colonial tenements are present. These are not tenements in the twentieth-century pejorative sense but in eighteenth-century parlance, meaning a house built as rental property.

Carpenter-builder James Verree acquired this land in 1754 and soon thereafter constructed a handsome Georgian single house of two and one-half stories. Thomas Heyward, American patriot, Revolutionary war officer, and a South Carolina signer of the Declaration of Independence, was a later nonresident owner.

Behind the house, almost invisible from the street, is one of Charleston's most enchanting walled gardens — the perfect setting for a spring garden luncheon. The "bones" of the garden were laid out years ago by landscape architect and garden historian Loutrell Briggs at the request of the present owner, herself a nationally recognized gardener. Over the years, the garden has been refined and rethought, this being occasionally necessitated by storms that marred an otherwise tranquil and serene oasis. Occupying a space that measures thirty by fifty feet, its careful planning gives the illusion of greater depth. Near the back of the garden, a delightful lead sculpture of a girl with a goose clad in ivy presides over a reflecting pool surrounded by mellow old Charleston brick. In spring it is ablaze with color as azaleas and flowering fruit trees complement the greenery of clipped Japanese boxwood.

Today's Charleston gardener is the inheritor of a rich Carolina gardening tradition. As early as 1732, Charles Pinckney advertized seeds imported from London, thus introducing the daisy, alyssum, periwinkle, foxglove, snapdragon, stock, thrift and violet. French botanist André Michaux, sent by his government in 1786 to cultivate plants for royal palaces, introduced the camellia, japonica, and ginkgo and candleberry trees. Other plants imported from the East included the mimosa, gardenia, crepe myrtle, tea olive and hydrangea. Carolina's native species, the dogwood, live oak, cassena, yellow jessamine and the magnificent magnolia grandiflora, were greatly admired by early visitors. They still are today as Charleston's gardens continue to be a source of pleasure for owners and visitors.

GARDEN LUNCHEON

Serves 6 to 8

White Wine Sangria
Cold Carrot Soup
Crab-Stuffed Chicken Breasts
Posh Asparagus
Melon Salad
Blueberry Muffins
Mrs. Scarborough's Green Tomato Pickles
Oatmeal Lace Cookies
Elegant Pears

White Wine Sangria
Yields 12 servings

1 cup strawberries
1 lime
1 apple
1 orange
2 fifths (6½ cups) dry white wine
1 cup orange juice
⅔ cup sugar
½ cup lime juice
¼ cup brandy
2 cups soda water

Hull and halve the strawberries. Thinly slice lime, apple and orange. In a large pitcher, combine white wine, orange juice, sugar, lime juice and brandy; stir until sugar dissolves. Add slices of fruit and chill for several hours. Just before serving, stir in soda water and pour over ice.

Cold Carrot Soup
Yields 6 to 8 servings

2 slices bacon
¼ cup onion, chopped
½ clove garlic, crushed
2 13¾-ounce cans chicken broth
1 cup carrots, peeled and sliced
½ cup potatoes, peeled and diced
1 small tomato, peeled and chopped
½ teaspoon salt
Dash white pepper
¼ cup sour cream
Chopped parsley for garnish
Toasted slivered almonds for garnish

In a 3-quart Dutch oven, cook bacon until crisp; remove from pot and drain. Sauté onion and garlic in bacon drippings until onion is transparent. Crumble bacon and add to onion mixture. Stir in remaining ingredients except sour cream, parsley and almonds. Heat to a boil; reduce heat. Simmer, uncovered, until vegetables are tender, about 15 to 20 minutes. Pour the mixture into a blender and cover; blend on high speed until smooth. (Blend in as many batches as necessary and then mix together.) If thinner soup is desired, chicken broth, milk or water may be added. Before serving, whip the sour cream into the soup. Garnish with chopped parsley and toasted almonds.

Crab-Stuffed Chicken Breasts
Yields 8 servings

8 chicken breasts, boned and skinned
3 tablespoons butter, divided
2 cups crabmeat
1 bunch green onions, chopped
4 ounces cream cheese, softened
1 teaspoon Worcestershire sauce
2 tablespoons dry white wine
Salt and pepper to taste
Slivered or sliced almonds for garnish,
   optional

Pound chicken breasts between wax paper until thin and flat. Set aside. Sauté the crab and onions in 2 tablespoons butter. Stir in cream cheese, Worcestershire, wine, salt and pepper. Divide crab mixture into 8 equal portions and place on chicken breasts. Roll and secure ends with toothpicks. Place breasts in buttered casserole. Melt remaining 1 tablespoon butter and brush on breasts. Bake at 350° for 45 minutes to 1 hour, uncovered. Spoon juice from pan over chicken breasts and sprinkle with toasted almonds if desired. To make this as shown in the picture, cut long, thin strips of green onion tops. Turn breast over, put strips in place; turn bundles over and tie strips on top.

Posh Asparagus
Yields 8 servings

1 15½-ounce can cut asparagus, drained
4 eggs
1 cup grated sharp Cheddar cheese
1 cup mayonnaise
1 cup condensed cream of mushroom soup
Salt and pepper to taste

Blend all ingredients in blender. Pour into a buttered 1½-quart soufflé dish. Place dish in ½ inch of water in a pan. Bake at 350° for 1½ hours.

Melon Salad
Yields 8 servings

1 honeydew melon
2 kiwi, peeled and thinly sliced
½ pound seedless red grapes; or fresh
    pineapple, cored, peeled and sliced

3 tablespoons fresh lime juice
2 tablespoons honey
Strawberries for garnish, optional

Scoop melon balls out of the honeydew. Combine melon, kiwi and grapes in a bowl. In another bowl mix lime juice and honey. Toss fruit mixture with the lime dressing and serve. May garnish with strawberries.

Blueberry Muffins
Yields 12 large or 24 small muffins

½ cup butter, softened
1 cup sugar
2 eggs
1 teaspoon vanilla
2 cups sifted flour
1½ teaspoons baking powder
¼ teaspoon salt
½ cup milk
1½ to 2 cups blueberries

Preheat oven to 375°. Grease or line muffin tins. In large bowl with mixer at high speed, beat butter with sugar, eggs and vanilla until light and fluffy. Sift together flour, baking powder and salt. At low speed, beat in flour mixture in fourths, alternating with milk in thirds. Beat until smooth. Gently fold in blueberries. Use ¼ to ½ cup batter for large muffins, 2 tablespoons batter for small muffins. Bake at 375°, 20 to 25 minutes for large muffins, 15 minutes for small, until golden brown.

Mrs. Scarborough's Green Tomato Pickles

Yields 14 half-pints

7 pounds green tomatoes, sliced
2 gallons water
3 cups powdered lime
5 pounds plus 1¼ cups sugar
3 pints plus ¾ cup cider vinegar
1¼ teaspoons ground cloves
1¼ teaspoons ginger
1¼ teaspoons allspice
1¼ teaspoons celery seed
1¼ teaspoons mace
1¼ teaspoons cinnamon
Green food coloring

Soak sliced tomatoes in lime water in a cooler for 24 hours. Drain. Soak in fresh water for 4 hours, changing water and rinsing tomatoes every half hour. Drain well. Make a syrup of sugar, vinegar and spices in a big pickling pot. Bring to a boil, then add tomatoes. Let this stand overnight. Next morning boil for an hour or until tomatoes are clear. Add green food coloring to the liquid. Boil pint jars in a separate pickling pot or sterilize jars in a dishwasher. Boil lids in a separate pot. Put tomatoes in jars and cover with liquid while hot. Place lids on jars; turn upside down to seal.

Oatmeal Lace Cookies

Yields 7 dozen cookies

2 cups quick oatmeal
2 cups sugar

4 heaping tablespoons flour
½ teaspoon salt
½ teaspoon baking powder
1 cup (2 sticks) butter, melted
2 eggs, beaten
2 teaspoons vanilla
6 ounces chocolate chips

Combine dry ingredients. Add butter and eggs. Mix well. Add vanilla and chocolate chips. Drop by the teaspoon onto baking sheets which have been lined with aluminum foil. Allow plenty of room for cookies to spread. Bake at 325° for 5 to 6 minutes or until cookies are golden. Remove pan from oven and set on rack to cool completely. Do not attempt to remove cookies until pan is cold. Cookies peel off easily when cooled thoroughly.

Elegant Pears

Yields 8 servings

8 large pears, all same size without
  blemishes or bruises
1¼ cups sugar
1 quart water
6 to 8 cloves
2 teaspoons lemon peel
1 cinnamon stick

Peel pears, leaving stem intact. Core from bottom, still leaving stem in place. In large saucepan, bring sugar, water, cloves, cinnamon stick and lemon peel to a boil. Boil for 10 minutes. Using slotted spoon, add 4 pears to liquid. Simmer until pears are slightly tender. Remove from poaching liquid and drain. Repeat process for remaining pears. Cool.

FILLING
½ cup chopped pecans
⅓ cup chopped dried currants
¼ cup dried, chopped apricots
3 tablespoons chopped dates
1 tablespoon brandy

Mix the above ingredients together. Gently and carefully stuff 1 tablespoon of filling mixture into the end of each pear.

GLAZE
12 ounces semisweet chocolate
2 tablespoons vegetable shortening

In double boiler, melt chocolate and shortening. Drain pears thoroughly and pat dry. Place pears on small wire rack. Pour chocolate into a container with a spout. Carefully pour chocolate over pears, one at a time. The entire pear can be covered or half the pear can be covered with the chocolate mixture. Chill pears for 30 minutes; serve within 4 to 6 hours.

FACING PAGE

Springtime garden luncheon graces the patio in the James Verree house garden. White Wine Sangria, Blueberry Muffins and Crab-Stuffed Chicken Breasts served on a wrought-iron garden table.

*Under a spreading live oak at Magnolia Plantation gardens,
a Lowcountry picnic is served in coiled sea-grass baskets.*

Afternoon Picnic
Magnolia Plantation Gardens

THE GARDENS at Magnolia Plantation on the Ashley River have been open to the public since 1870. In 1875, *Harper's New Monthly Magazine* wrote of Magnolia,

> In the spring, when a little paddle-wheel steamer carries tourists up the Ashley . . . , many of the visitors go no further than this enchanting garden, where they wander through the glowing aisles of azaleas and forget the lapse of time, recalled from their trance of enjoyment only by the whistle of the boat, which carries them back to the city. . . .

Magnolia was the first seat of the Drayton family in South Carolina. English-born Thomas Drayton, Jr., the progenitor of the family in America, had arrived in Carolina by way of Barbadoes as early as 1671. Receiving the property through the dowry of his Barbadian wife Ann Fox, Drayton built one of the first mansions of consequence in the colony. This was replaced in the early nineteenth century by a large frame house which met a fiery end in 1865 at the hands of General Sherman's troops. The present structure was moved to the site in 1873 by the Reverend John Grimke-Drayton, the wealthy inheritor of the property, who had been reduced to near poverty by the Civil War. Undaunted, he moved the family's pre-Revolutionary summer house from Summerville to the plantation by barge and re-erected it on the charred foundations of his former mansion. It remains as a family home and a testament to the realities of plantation life in the later nineteenth century.

The lush gardens at Magnolia are largely the creation of the Reverend Grimke-Drayton. Inheriting the property at age 22, following the accidental shooting of his elder brother Thomas during a deer hunt, he devoted himself to the embellishment of the plantation's natural beauty. John Grimke-Drayton had entered the Episcopal seminary in New York in 1838 and shortly thereafter had married Julia Ewing, daughter of a prominent Philadelphia attorney. His passion for gardening may have been linked to his wife's homesickness. In a letter to a fellow clergyman in Philadelphia, he expressed his desire "to create an earthly paradise in which my dear Julia may forever forget Philadelphia and her desire to return there."

Eschewing the formality of the French-inspired parterred gardens which had influenced the gardens at nearby Middleton Place a century earlier, Grimke-Drayton played up the romantic aspects of the landscape, incorporating existing moss-hung cypress and dark ponds into the garden scheme. The azaleas he introduced to America join his early use of the camellia japonica to create an enchanted and colorful woodland.

The informality of this romantic garden calls for an informal country picnic of fried chicken and potato salad served from Lowcountry sea-grass baskets. The coiled baskets are part of an Afro-American folk-art craft tradition that has survived in Carolina for over three hundred years. Initially they were made from black rush bound with oak splits or palmetto stems cut into strips; sweetgrass sewn with palmetto leaf has been employed in more recent times.

Slaves from the rice growing regions of Africa were an important factor in the success of rice cultivation in early Carolina. The fanner basket, a large shallow winnowing tray, was an important tool in production; it was used to throw the threshed and pounded grain into the air, allowing the wind to blow away the chaff. The coiled basketry tradition has survived the loss of its older function to form an indigenous and decorative link to Carolina's economic and craft origins.

THEY make no beer of malt in Carolina, but they make some of molasses and also of percymon both which are much inferior to good English beer, and as it won't keep is only made and expended in the winter season but Charles Town is very well supplied with porter from England at 9 shillings per dozen bottles, which is commonly drank by most people of property at meals or else weak grog or rum punch, for they always can buy the best Jamaica rum from 2s 8d to 3s 6d a gallon by the puncheon or hogshead. French claret is also to be drank much cheaper than in England, but other wines are in general almost as dear.

"Charleston, S.C., in 1774 as Described by an English Traveller"

AFTERNOON PICNIC

Serves 4

Shandy Gaff
Antipasto Tray
Fried Chicken
Dill–Sour Cream Potato Salad
Hearty Coleslaw
Green Beans à la Rouge
Evan's Bread Sticks
Cheddar Cheese Spread
Fruit Tarts

Shandy Gaff

Yields 2 servings

1 beer
1 ginger beer
2 wedges lime, plus additional for garnish,
    if desired

Pour equal portions of regular beer and ginger beer into old fashioned glass. Squeeze one lime wedge into each glass. Stir, add ice, garnish with additional lime slices and serve.

Antipasto Tray

Yields 6 to 12 servings

1 6-ounce jar marinated artichoke hearts,
    drained, liquid reserved
1 6-ounce can ripe olives, drained
1 7-ounce jar large pimento-stuffed green
    olives
1 pint cherry tomatoes
6 eggs, hard cooked and quartered
8 ounces pepperoni, sliced thin
8 ounces feta cheese

Arrange the first 6 ingredients in a spoke pattern on round tray. Crumble half the feta cheese and mix with reserved marinade and sprinkle over the black olives and tomatoes. Cube remaining cheese and outline sections with squares of cheese. Serve with toothpicks.

Fried Chicken

Yields 9 to 10 pieces

9 to 10 pieces of chicken
2½ cups flour
4 teaspoons salt, divided
2 teaspoons pepper
Vegetable shortening for frying

Wash chicken. Add 2 teaspoons salt to enough cold water to cover chicken; soak chicken for 1 hour. Pat dry. Combine flour, remaining salt and pepper in a bag. Add chicken one piece at a time and shake until coated with the seasoned flour. Fill frying pan three-fourths full with shortening and heat on high until hot. Place chicken in pan and cook approximately 8 minutes, or until one side is partly brown. Lower heat to medium and turn chicken to other side. Cook another 5 minutes. Turn back to first side. Check to be sure chicken is browned equally on both sides; adjust temperature if shortening becomes too hot, and add more shortening if necessary. Total cooking time is approximately 20 minutes.

Dill–Sour Cream
Potato Salad

Yields 6 servings

3 pounds new potatoes
⅓ cup white vinegar
¼ cup chopped onion
2 teaspoons salt

Continued . . .

1 teaspoon sugar
1 teaspoon dried dill weed
Freshly ground pepper to taste
1 cup sour cream
3 hard-cooked eggs, optional

Cook unpeeled potatoes until tender in enough water to cover. Cool and slice thinly into large bowl. In a small bowl, combine vinegar, onion, salt, sugar, dill weed and pepper. Pour over potatoes and toss evenly to coat. Cover bowl and chill 8 hours, or up to 24 hours. Before serving, gently fold in sour cream. Optional: 3 hard-cooked eggs, chopped, may be added with the sour cream.

Hearty Coleslaw
Yields 4 to 5 servings

1 pound celery cabbage (Napa), shredded
¼ pound blue cheese, crumbled
2½ tablespoons cider vinegar
⅛ teaspoon dry mustard
½ teaspoon celery seeds
½ to 1 garlic clove, minced
½ teaspoon salt
¼ teaspoon white pepper
1 tablespoon sugar
3 tablespoons minced onion
⅓ cup safflower oil
4 to 5 bell pepper cups

In large bowl, toss together the cabbage and blue cheese; cover and chill for 1 hour. While cabbage mixture is chilling, whisk together in a bowl the vinegar, mustard, celery seeds, garlic, salt, pepper, sugar, onion and oil until emulsified. Chill dressing. Just before serving, pour dressing over cabbage mixture and toss gently. Serve in bell pepper cups; garnish with extra blue cheese if desired.

Green Beans à la Rouge
Yields 4 servings

½ cup red bell pepper cut into
   ⅛-by-3-inch strips
1 teaspoon balsamic vinegar
1 tablespoon butter
Freshly ground black pepper to taste
1 pound fresh green beans

In saucepan over medium heat, melt butter. Add red pepper and gently stir until tender, several minutes. Add vinegar to pepper and set aside. Microwave green beans 3 to 5 minutes until crisp-tender. Just before serving, combine green beans with red pepper mixture, tossing lightly. This dish may be served hot or cold.

Evan's Bread Sticks
Yields 14 bread sticks

2 tablespoons warm water
1 package yeast
1 cup warm water
4 to 4½ cups flour
2½ tablespoons sugar

2 tablespoons caraway seeds
1½ teaspoons salt
½ teaspoon garlic powder
1 tablespoon oil

Soften yeast in 2 tablespoons warm water. In food processor, using steel blade, blend yeast mixture with warm water. Add rest of ingredients making a stiff dough. Knead in food processor until dough is smooth and elastic and leaves the side of the bowl. Roll or pat dough into a rectangle, 6 by 21 inches; cut into strips, ½ by 6 inches. Twist each strip to form sticks; place on greased cookie sheet. Cover with plastic wrap. Let rise in warm place for 1 hour or until doubled in bulk. Bake at 400° for 15 minutes or until light brown. Sprinkle extra caraway seeds or coarse salt on bread before baking.

Cheddar Cheese Spread

Yields 1 cup

½ pound sharp Cheddar cheese, grated
1 teaspoon garlic juice
Dash cayenne pepper
1 tablespoon Worcestershire sauce
½ teaspoon dry mustard
¼ cup flat beer

Combine all ingredients, mixing until smooth. Refrigerate. This spread will keep for several weeks. Take out of refrigerator 30 minutes before serving.

Fruit Tarts

Yields 12 small tarts

12 Tart Shells
½ pint fresh raspberries or other fruit
6 slices kiwi fruit, cut in half, optional
Apricot Glaze

Place Tart Shell on flat surface; spread inside of tart with a thin layer of Apricot Glaze. Carefully place a row of raspberries clockwise at an angle. Place another row of raspberries conterclockwise at an angle. Continue until the tart is filled with raspberries. Spread a thin layer of Apricot Glaze on top to hold raspberries. A slice of kiwi may be placed in the center if desired. Carefully pour 1 to 2 tablespoons of remaining glaze over tarts. Refrigerate until ready to serve.

TART SHELLS

1 cup finely ground almonds
1 cup flour
¼ cup sugar
½ teaspoon baking powder
Pinch salt
¼ cup (½ stick) butter, cut into pieces
1 egg, lightly beaten

In food processor, using steel blade, combine almonds, flour, sugar, baking powder, salt and butter. Process until mixture resembles corn meal. Add egg; process until dough forms a ball. Remove from processor bowl and chill 1 hour in refrigerator.

Continued . . .

To make tart shells: Divide dough into 12 equal portions; press dough into tart pans which are 2 inches in diameter. Flute edges if preferred. Place in freezer until dough feels firm. Remove and bake at 350° for 15 to 20 minutes until lightly browned. Remove from oven and set aside to cool. When ready to fill, lift tart shell from pan, transfer it to a flat serving dish, and add raspberries or fruit of your choice. Strawberries, grapes or other fresh fruit work well.

APRICOT GLAZE
1½ cups apricot preserves
1 envelope unflavored gelatin
¼ cup cold water
3 tablespoons kirsch or apricot brandy

In a small saucepan, over low to medium heat, melt the preserves until it is liquid. In a small bowl, add gelatin to water and kirsch. Stir to dissolve. Bring preserves to a boil; add gelatin mixture, stirring until completely dissolved. Simmer for a few minutes; remove from heat. Process in food processor until smooth. This mixture may need to be reheated if not used immediately.

McKenzie and McNeill

Arrived from Bourdeaux, the *Northward.*
CHEESE—3000 wt. American Cheefe, almoft equal to Englifh.
FRUITS—Green Gages, Apricots, Peaches and Pears nicely preferved in Brandy and Syrup.
SPICES—Mafe, Nutmeg, Cloves, and Cinnamon, Pimento, Ginger, Bengal Curre Powder, with the receipt for ufing it. A few boxes of real Spanifh SEGARS.

Charleston Courier
February 12, 1804

A Charleston Breakfast
The Edmondston-Alston House

IN 1838, wealthy Georgetown County rice planter Charles Alston purchased this handsome mansion on East Battery for use as his town house. As the social and economic center for the Carolina Lowcountry, Charleston was a mecca for South Carolina planters who maintained city mansions in addition to their plantation holdings. The house had been completed ten years earlier by Charles Edmondston, a merchant and wharf owner. Sadly, the great panic of 1837 brought financial reverses to Edmondston and he was forced to sell his new house in order to pay his creditors.

Alston's family had arrived in Carolina shortly after the initial 1670 settlement and had prospered with the success of rice cultivation. Charles Alston's substantial riches enabled him to redecorate the original late Federal house, bringing it in step with the taste for Greek revival through the addition of piazzas with classical columns and a parapet with the family's crest proudly displayed on the eastern facade. Today, it is owned by a descendant and is open to visitors under the auspices of the Middleton Place Foundation.

The Alstons were lovers of the turf, Charles' father, William, having been among the organizers of the fourth South Carolina Jockey Club in 1792. The fashionable new Washington Race course was opened in 1793 in the area now occupied by Hampton Park and race week in February became the most social week of the Charleston year.

Accompanying the races was a round of parties and balls to which plantation society flocked. Mrs. Charles Alston (Emma Clara Pringle) apparently gave the most brilliant ball of the 1851 season. On February 18, 1851, Mrs. Charles Sinkler wrote to her father in Philadelphia after her return to the country from town, " . . . We were invited also to a ball at Mrs. Charles Alston's, an aunt of Lizzie Middleton's husband which I heard was the handsomest ever given in Charleston. . . ." A record of this extraordinary affair survives in Mrs. Alston's own cookbook:

For our Ball of 1851

18 dozen plates; 14 dozen knives; 28 dozen spoons; 6 dozen wine glasses; As many champaigne (sic) glasses as could be collected; 4 wild turkeys; 4 hams — 2 for sandwiches & 2 for the supper tables; 8 pates; 60 partridges; 6 pr of Pheasants; 6 pr Canvassback Ducks; 5 pr of our wild ducks; 8 Charlotte Russes; 4 Pyramids — 2 of crystalized fruit & 2 of Cocoanut; 4 Orange baskets; 4 Italian Creams; an immense quantity of bonbons; 7 dozen Cocoanut rings; 7 dozen Kiss cakes; 7 dozen Macaroons; 4 moulds of Jelly; 4 of Bavarian cream; 3 dollars worth of celery & lettuce; 10 quarts of Oysters; 4 cakes of chocolate; coffee; 4 small black cakes. . . .

On such an occasion as this, the sliding pocket doors with their silver hardware would have recessed into the walls and the double drawing rooms would become a spacious ballroom. We show the front drawing room in a more intimate mood — set for breakfast with a riverfront view — as the sun rises over the Cooper River.

THE butter commonly used in Carolina is very much like what is called the best cambridge in England which is to be had from 4d to 6d a pound. Fresh butter which is not often to be had in Charles Town is never under a shilling a pound and not very good neither. Eggs are commonly about 8 a groat. Peas and beans from 6d to a shilling a peck and vegitables of all kinds at much the same price as they are commonly sold for in and about London. The bread which is very good is generally sold at the rate of about 6d or 7d the quartern loaf. Most kinds of fruits (gooseberries and currants excepted) grow here as in England tho' not so plenty nor so good flavor'd in general but I am informed the northern colonies produce all kinds of English fruits in great abundance, which are reckoned full as good flavor'd as any in England. China oranges grow in Carolina, but rather scarce and not kindly, for now and then a little severer winter than usual cuts most of them off. However it is pretty well supplied with them, lemons and limes from a place called Providence, so that they have them in Charles Town very fresh and good most part of the year. They also have from the same place plenty of pine apples one half the year from 4d to 8d a piece, which are in general exceeding fine flavor'd.

"Charleston, S.C., in 1774 as Described by an English Traveller"

Virginia Mountain Butter:

A FEW Firkins for ſale — Apply to Capt. Pope, on bard the ſchooner *Frederickſburg,* at BEAL'S WHARF.

The Times, Charleston
April 8, 1808

Cheeſes and Hams

A Few Engliſh CHEESES juſt arrived, and for ſale. Alſo, Boſton BACON HAMS, of a ſuperior quality, juſt landed and for ſale, by

McKenzie & McNeill

The Times, Charleston
April 8, 1808

A CHARLESTON BREAKFAST

Serves 6

Champagne Cordials
Green Parmesan Tomatoes
Baked Hominy with Cheese
Baked Apples with Sausage Stuffing
Sautéed Shrimp
Mrs. Bremer's Coffee Cake • Sally Lunn
Pear Honey • Peach Preserves
Seasoned Coffee

Champagne Cordials

Yields 6 servings

3 cups orange juice, chilled
3 cups pineapple juice, chilled
3 cups champagne, chilled
6 orange peel strips

Mix orange juice and pineapple juice together. Add champagne. Pour into champagne or wine glasses and top each with orange-peel strip.

Green Parmesan Tomatoes

Yields 6 servings

¾ cup flour
1 cup dry bread crumbs
½ cup grated Parmesan cheese
½ teaspoon dried thyme
½ teaspoon crushed red pepper flakes
1 pound green tomatoes, cored and sliced
  ¼ to ⅓ inch thick
¼ teaspoon salt
¼ teaspoon freshly ground black pepper
2 eggs, lightly beaten
⅓ cup olive oil

Put flour in small bowl. In another bowl, stir together the bread crumbs, Parmesan cheese, thyme, red pepper flakes, salt and pepper until combined. Working with one tomato slice at a time, dredge in flour, dip in beaten eggs and then coat with the bread crumb mixture. In a large heavy skillet, heat the olive oil. Sauté each tomato slice for 1 to 2 minutes on each side or until golden. Transfer to heated platter using a slotted spatula. Serve immediately.

Baked Hominy with Cheese

Yields 8 servings

1 cup white or yellow grits
1 teaspoon salt
1 cup grated Cheddar cheese
½ cup grated Parmesan cheese
½ cup (1 stick) margarine
½ cup milk
2 beaten eggs
1 clove garlic, minced
1 dash hot sauce

Cook grits in 4 cups boiling water to which the salt has been added. When mixture has thickened, add cheeses, margarine, milk, eggs, garlic and hot sauce. Stir until cheese is melted; pour into greased 2-quart casserole. Bake at 350° for 1 hour.

Baked Apples with Sausage Stuffing

Yields 8 servings

8 apples
1 pound bulk sausage
1 small red onion, chopped
Salt to taste

Slice top off apples and remove core, leaving a shell ½ to ¾ thick. Chop apple tops and any other edible pulp before discarding cores. Mix chopped apple, sausage and onion.

Sprinkle inside of apples with salt, then fill with sausage mixture. Bake at 350° for 30 to 45 minutes.

Sautéed Shrimp

Yields 6 to 8 servings

4 tablespoons butter
2 pounds shrimp, peeled and deveined
1 clove garlic, minced
Salt and pepper to taste
Paprika, optional

Just before serving, melt butter in medium-size frying pan. Add garlic and sauté lightly. Add shrimp, cooking 2 to 4 minutes until pink, stirring occasionally. If serving this dish at lunch or dinner, ½ to 1 teaspoon of Worcestershire and ¼ to ½ teaspoon of red pepper flakes will add a lot of zip.

Mrs. Bremer's Coffee Cake

Yields 12 slices

½ cup packed light brown sugar
1½ cups plus 2 tablespoons flour, divided
2 teaspoons cinnamon
¼ cup (½ stick) butter or margarine, melted

½ cup chopped pecans
3 teaspoons baking powder
½ teaspoon salt
¾ cup white sugar
¼ cup vegetable shortening
1 egg, beaten
½ cup milk
1 teaspoon vanilla

Combine brown sugar, 2 tablespoons flour, cinnamon, butter and pecans; set aside. Sift together 1½ cups flour, baking powder, salt and ¾ cup white sugar. Cut in shortening. Add beaten egg, milk and vanilla. In a greased 8-inch square pan, spread half of cake batter. Sprinkle with half of pecan mixture, and cover with remaining batter. Top with remaining pecan mixture. Bake at 350° for 30 minutes.

Sally Lunn

Yields 16 slices

4½ cups flour
⅓ cup sugar
1 teaspoon salt
1 package dry, active yeast
1¼ cups milk
½ cup (1 stick) margarine
3 eggs, beaten

Combine 2 cups flour, sugar, salt and yeast in large bowl. Stir well. Heat milk and margarine in microwave for 45 seconds or until margarine is melted. Gradually add to dry ingredients, beating at low speed. Add eggs and remaining flour. Mix well; cover and let rise 1 hour or until doubled in bulk. Stir down and spoon into greased and floured 10-inch tube pan. Cover and let rise until double (about 1 hour). Bake at 400° for 50 minutes. Serve warm with butter and your favorite preserves. Toast leftovers for breakfast or snacks.

Pear Honey
Yields 4 to 6 half-pints

8 to 9 large ripe pears, cored and ground in
*   food processor*
1 pint applesauce
2½ cups sugar
1 10½-ounce can crushed pineapple

Combine pears, applesauce and sugar in heavy saucepan. Cook mixture for 1 hour, stirring often. Mixture needs to be thick so it may need to cook longer. Add pineapple and cook over low heat for 30 minutes. Spices may be added if desired. Pour into sterilized jars and seal.

Peach Preserves
Yields 6 half-pints

5 cups ripe peaches, peeled and sliced
2½ cups sugar

Mix sliced peaches and sugar together. Stir and let sit overnight. Next morning, cook over medium heat 30 minutes, or longer if you prefer. Pour into hot jars and seal.

Seasoned Coffee
Yields 8 servings

½ teaspoon cinnamon
½ teaspoon freshly ground nutmeg
6 tablespoons coffee

Add cinnamon and nutmeg to top of coffee in percolator or filter basket; perk or drip-brew as usual. For a full-bodied brew, use 2 tablespoons of coffee for each 8 ounces of water.

FACING PAGE

A breakfast of shrimp and hominy at the Edmondston-Alston house. The table is set with old Canton china.

A buffet table in the garden of George W. Williams' coach house features local delicacies at a spring christening party.

Assorted Fruits garnished with azalea blossoms and Rosettes accompany Granpa Schachte's Punch.

Shrimp, Meatballs and Snow Peas in a chafing dish complement Benne Cheese Biscuits and Cherry Tomatoes Stuffed with Crabmeat and Cream Cheese.

Christening Party
The George Williams Coach House

CHARLESTON CHILDREN are introduced to the joys of antiquities at a very early age. A baptism in one of the city's historic churches often includes the use of a cherished family christening bowl and almost certainly an antique christening gown handed down lovingly from generation to generation. Such practices are not unusual in a city where preservation is a life-style.

In similar fashion, many of Charleston's historic buildings have been recycled over the years to make them viable for succeeding generations. The concept is known as "adaptive use," and its success in Charleston is a credit to the imagination and determination of preservationists and private property owners. Solutions have included the conversion of old dwellings into banks or stores, the remodeling of warehouses into dwellings, and the adaptation of historic commercial buildings for use as law offices and restaurants. This practice has proved imperative in preserving the historic character of neighborhoods and the scale and harmony of streetscapes. Some would argue that the local practice goes back to the early nineteenth century when the Manigault family adapted the old powder magazine, an arsenal for the early province's gunpowder, for use as their wine cellar.

A particularly successful and handsome example of adaptive use is this house on lower Church Street, once the coach house for George W. Williams' imposing Calhoun mansion on Meeting Street. The property was divided and purchased by previous owners in 1940 and the redundant coach house was transformed into a spacious and stately residence.

When built for horses and carriages in the 1870's, the southern facade had two double doors and an earthen floor. Six horse stalls were located on the northern side. The upper story was used as a hayloft with lodging for a groom and a coachman. The whole overlooked an active stable yard.

It is quieter now, the stable yard having been transformed into a handsome walled garden incorporating the original eastern brick stable wall. Where horses were once shod, azaleas and camellias now thrive. Fig vine, wisteria and yellow Lady Banksia roses trail over the garden walls.

From the drawing room and dining room, three pairs of glazed double doors open onto a terrace of old Charleston bricks, shaded by a large live oak planted when it was the size of a buggy whip. A delicate wrought-iron balcony above the central bay gives the house additional architectural character and provides the perfect vantage point from which to survey the garden. Across the street, the stately piazzas of the George Holmes house offer a scenic vista.

Arranged on a table in the garden, this christening party is a Sunday afternoon celebration following the service. Under sunny skies and amid relatives and friends, the new Charlestonian is introduced to the pleasures of life in the restored historic city.

CHRISTENING PARTY

Serves 12

Granpa Schachte's Punch
Rita's Cheese Log
Watercress Tea Sandwiches
Benne Cheese Biscuits
Asparagus Spears with Sour Cream–Dill Dip
Roast Beef Spirals
Shrimp, Meatballs and Snow Peas in Chafing Dish
Stuffed Cherry Tomatoes with
Cream Cheese or Crabmeat Filling
Assorted Fruits and Dipping Sauces
Strawberry Beignets
Drop Brownies • Rosettes

Granpa Schachte's Punch

Yields 1 gallon

2 quarts strong tea
2 quarts bourbon
Juice of 2 lemons (or more to taste)
2 cups sugar

Pour tea, bourbon and lemon juice into container. Add sugar, stirring until sugar is dissolved. Chill several hours. Serve over ice.

Rita's Cheese Log

Yields 2½ cups

12 ounces cream cheese, softened
½ pound extra-sharp Cheddar cheese, grated
1 large onion, grated
Dash red pepper
Salt and freshly ground pepper to taste
¾ cup chopped pecans, divided
2 red pepper strips for garnish, ¼ inch wide

In a large bowl, mix together cheeses, onion, red pepper, salt and pepper with ¼ cup pecans. Shape into a log 2 inches in diameter. Chill for 1 hour. To decorate for serving, place red pepper strips diagonally across log, dividing it into thirds. Sprinkle remaining ½ cup nuts on end sections, being careful not to spill any on middle section. Decorate center section with fancy radish. Serve with assorted crackers.

Watercress Tea Sandwiches

Yields 24 small sandwiches

1½ cups chopped watercress
2 tablespoons chopped green onion
¼ teaspoon white pepper
¼ teaspoon salt
3 ounces cream cheese, room temperature
2 tablespoons sour cream
1 loaf firm white bread with crusts removed, thinly sliced

Mix together watercress, green onion, pepper, salt, cream cheese and sour cream until thoroughly blended. Spread slice of bread with a thin layer of mixture; top with a slice of bread. Cut into strips or triangles. These can also be served open-faced. (If sandwiches will not be served immediately, be sure to butter each side of bread before assembling.)

Benne Cheese Biscuits

Yields 3 dozen

¼ cup (½ stick) cold butter, cut into pieces
¼ pound sharp Cheddar cheese, grated
½ cup flour
½ teaspoon salt
Dash cayenne pepper
½ cup toasted benne seeds or sesame seeds

Combine butter, cheese, flour, salt and cayenne in food processor and blend until a ball is formed. Remove from the processor and work the benne seeds into the dough by hand. Roll into a long roll, approximately 1 to 1¼ inches in diameter. Wrap in wax paper and chill at least 3 hours. Slice thinly (¼ inch) and bake on ungreased baking sheet at 375° for 9 to 11 minutes.

Asparagus Spears with Sour Cream–Dill Dip

Yields 12 servings

3 to 4 pounds fresh asparagus
6 quarts water
1 teaspoon salt
½ lemon, squeezed
Sour Cream–Dill Dip

Snap tough ends from asparagus. Bring water, salt and lemon to a rapid boil. Drop in asparagus and allow to boil 4 to 5 minutes or until desired tenderness is achieved. Remove from boiling water and plunge immediately into ice water. Drain on absorbent towels and chill until ready to serve. Best flavor if used the same day.

SOUR CREAM–DILL DIP
Yields 2 cups

1 egg
½ to 1 teaspoon salt
Dash of freshly ground black pepper
⅛ teaspoon sugar
4 teaspoons lemon juice
1 teaspoon grated onion
3 tablespoons finely chopped dill
1½ cups sour cream

Beat egg until fluffy and lemon colored. Add remaining ingredients in the order listed. Stir well. Chill. Serve with blanched asparagus, snow peas or any other spring vegetable.

Roast Beef Spirals

Yields 20

8 ounces cream cheese, softened
8 ounces sour cream
¼ cup horseradish
4 teaspoons Dijon mustard
Salt and pepper to taste
1 pound thinly sliced peppered roast beef

Mix cream cheese, sour cream, horseradish, mustard and seasonings until smooth. Spread on individual slices of roast beef. Roll each slice tightly beginning with long side. Refrigerate 3 hours or overnight. Remove and serve as is, or freeze for one hour to slice and serve in pinwheels.

Shrimp, Meatballs and Snow Peas in Chafing Dish

MEATBALLS
Yields 30 to 40 meatballs

2 slices bread, finely crumbled
1 teaspoon salt
1¼ teaspoons chili powder

Continued . . .

2 tablespoons milk
1 small egg, beaten
3 tablespoons finely chopped onion
1 tablespoon butter
1 pound lean ground beef

Combine bread crumbs, salt, chili powder, milk, egg and ground beef; set aside. Sauté onion in butter. Add beef mixture and combine thoroughly. Shape mixture into balls the size of walnuts. Place one layer deep in a shallow baking dish. Bake uncovered at 400° for 20 to 25 minutes or until browned. Remove from oven and drain off excess fat. Set aside.

SNOW PEAS

1½ pounds snow peas

String snow peas. Put in a shallow bowl. Microwave for 1 to 2 minutes. Cover and set aside.

SHRIMP

1 to 2 pounds shrimp, cooked, shelled and deveined

CHUTNEY SAUCE

1 9-ounce jar chutney
1½ cups sour cream

Mix the chutney and sour cream together. Refrigerate.

To assemble using a chafing dish: Wrap each meatball with a snow pea. Secure with a toothpick. Wrap each shrimp with a snow pea. Secure with a toothpick. Set aside. Heat chutney sauce mixture; place in chafing dish. Arrange meatballs and shrimp on top of sauce, with toothpick pointing out.

To assemble using a platter: Heat chutney mixture to room temperature. Place in small bowl in center of large platter. Arrange meatballs, shrimp and snow peas around bowl of sauce.

Stuffed Cherry Tomatoes
Yields 30

30 cherry tomatoes, same size if possible

Wash and dry tomatoes. Remove a thin slice from the bottom end of each tomato. Remove seeds and pulp. Put tomatoes on a rack, cut side down, to drain. Refrigerate until ready to use. Stuff with Cream Cheese or Crabmeat Filling, or your favorite mixture.

Cream Cheese Filling
Yields ¾ cup

3 ounces cream cheese, softened
¼ cup cream
¼ cup grated Parmesan cheese
1 tablespoon grated onion
½ teaspoon Worcestershire sauce

In food processor, blend cream cheese and cream. Add cheese, onion and Worcestershire and blend until smooth.

Crabmeat Filling
Yields ¾ cup

3 to 4 ounces crabmeat
¼ cup finely chopped celery
2 tablespoons chopped onion
⅛ teaspoon minced garlic
1 tablespoon mayonnaise
Salt and pepper to taste
½ tablespoon lemon juice
⅛ teaspoon curry powder, optional

In bowl, mix crabmeat, celery, onion and garlic. In another bowl, blend together mayonnaise, salt and pepper, lemon juice and curry powder. Toss crabmeat with mayonnaise mixture.

Assorted Fruits and Dipping Sauces

Arrange your favorite fruits on a platter or tray and serve one or more of the following dipping sauces in a scooped-out melon half.

Pineapple-Ginger Dipping Sauce
Yields 2 cups

8 ounces cream cheese, softened
1 10½-ounce can crushed pineapple, drained
¼ cup sour cream
¼ cup candied ginger, chopped

Using a food processor with steel blade, process the above ingredients until smooth. Refrigerate.

Lowcountry Fruit Sauce
Yields 2 cups

1½ tablespoons celery seed
⅓ cup sugar
¼ teaspoon dry mustard
½ teaspoon paprika
½ teaspoon salt
⅔ cup applesauce
¼ cup honey
3 tablespoons lemon juice
1 tablespoon vinegar
¼ teaspoon lemon rind
⅓ cup oil

Put the above ingredients into a food processor or blender. Blend until smooth. Chill.

Elegant Fruit Dip
Yields 2 cups

1 tablespoon butter
1 tablespoon flour
⅓ cup sugar
1½ tablespoons lemon juice
2 tablespoons orange juice
½ cup unsweetened pineapple juice
1 egg, beaten
½ cup whipping cream, whipped

Over medium heat in medium saucepan, melt butter and stir in flour to make a roux. Add sugar, lemon juice, orange juice and pineapple juice. Stir with wire whisk until mixture begins to thicken. Remove from heat. Add small amount of mixture to beaten egg, stir, then carefully add the egg mixture to hot mixture. Cool for a few minutes. Fold in whipped cream. This is an excellent sauce for fresh fruit and other desserts.

Strawberry Beignets
Yields 32

32 large strawberries
1 cup flour
1 teaspoon baking powder
1 teaspoon sugar
½ teaspoon salt
1 egg, separated
½ cup milk
1 tablespoon oil
Vegetable oil for frying
Powdered sugar

Wash and dry strawberries and remove caps. Sift flour, baking powder, sugar and salt. Beat egg yolk lightly; add milk and oil. Stir together flour and milk mixtures. Beat egg white until stiff. Fold into batter. Dip strawberries into batter; allow excess to drip off, and drop into oil heated to 375°. Fry until lightly browned. Remove from oil with slotted spoon and drain on paper towels. Roll in powdered sugar and serve at once. There are never enough.

Drop Brownies
Yields 24 large cookies

2 4-ounce packages German sweet chocolate
1 tablespoon butter
2 eggs
¾ cup sugar
¼ cup unsifted flour
¼ teaspoon baking powder
¼ teaspoon cinnamon
⅛ teaspoon salt
½ teaspoon vanilla extract
¾ cup chopped pecans

In a double boiler, melt chocolate and butter over hot water. Stir and cool. Beat eggs with an electric mixer until foamy. Add sugar, two tablespoons at a time, beating until thickened and no longer grainy. This takes about 5 minutes. Beat chocolate into egg mixture. Mix dry ingredients together and blend into batter. Stir in vanilla and nuts. Drop by teaspoonsful onto greased baking sheet. Bake at 350° until cookies feel set when lightly touched, about 8 to 10 minutes. These cookies crumble easily, so handle carefully.

Rosettes
Yields 3 dozen

2 eggs
1 tablespoon sugar
⅛ teaspoon salt
1 cup milk
1 cup flour

1 teaspoon vanilla extract
Vegetable oil or shortening for frying
Confectioners' sugar for dusting

In small, deep bowl, beat eggs with sugar and salt. Add milk, flour and vanilla. Beat until consistency is even and smooth. Heat oil or shortening in deep saucepan or deep fat fryer to 365° degrees. Heat rosette iron in fat for several minutes. Dip iron into batter, making certain the batter does not come to the top of the iron (leave at least ⅛ inch so that rosette will be easy to remove from iron). Dip iron again into batter to insure an even coat.

Lower iron into hot fat and cook until rosette is a delicate brown. Lift iron and remove rosette to brown craft paper or paper towels to drain. Rosette can be loosened from iron with a dinner fork if necessary. Immediately repeat dipping and cooking, remembering always to have iron hot before dipping into batter. After rosettes have drained, dust with powdered sugar. Store in tightly covered container. Batter may be stored several days in refrigerator.

The rosette iron can be purchased in the gourmet cooking section of department stores.

Received

Per the fchooner Experiment, Wm. Taylor, Mufter, from Jamaica,

A few hhds. of PRIME SUGARS,
JAMAICA RUM,
GINGER, in bags,
PIMENTO, in barrels,
ORANGES and LIMES,
Which will be fold upon very reafonable terms.
Apply to

TUNNO & COX

Charleston Courier
February 12, 1804

Spoleto Fete
The William Gibbes House

CHARLESTON has long been attractive to artists. In December 1838, English actress Fanny Kemble visited the city during an American tour and was charmed. "The appearance of the city is highly picturesque, a word which can apply to none other of the American towns; and although the place is certainly pervaded with an air of decay, it is a genteel infirmity, as might be that of a distressed elderly gentlewoman. It has none of the smug mercantile primness of the Northern cities, but a look of state, as of quondam wealth and importance, a little gone down in the world, yet remembering still its former dignity." Kemble found the city to have a European air, noting, "in one street you seem to be in an old English town, and in another in some continental city of France or Italy."

One hundred and thirty-nine years later, Gian Carlo Menotti was no doubt taken with these same Old World aspects and Charleston was selected from among several American cities to play host to the distinguished Spoleto Festival U.S.A. Each year, for two full weeks in late May and early June, the entire city becomes a stage for Spoleto, America's most comprehensive arts festival. Like Salzburg, Edinburgh and Bath, the ambience of Charleston is particularly suited to a festival atmosphere. The city's parks, historic churches, concert halls and theatres provide a variety of venues for a dazzling array of opera, dance, theatre, chamber music, and choral and orchestral concerts.

Parties abound during Spoleto, from opening night's formal gala to more intimate outdoor gatherings. This Spoleto fete is set in the expansive garden of the William Gibbes house, built in 1772 by a wealthy Charleston merchant. The sober, symmetrical Georgian facade on South Battery gives little hint of the splendors that await the visitor in the garden. An entrance hall of ballroom proportions bisects the house and provides access to the garden, which is entered by descending a double set of curving stone steps. Shaded by ancient live oaks veiled in Spanish moss, a paved walk flanked by vine-covered brick piers leads to a swimming pool disguised as a garden pond. Beyond this, a grassy lawn encircles a fishpond. There is also a formal parterred rose garden and an herb garden adjacent to the dependency, which served as a kitchen in William Gibbes' day.

In one corner, it is easy to imagine oneself in the garden of a French chateau; in another, an Italian villa. The present garden scheme was devised sixty years ago by Loutrell Briggs, who made use of the existing evidence of earlier gardens on the site. Today, his creation has matured and acquired an antiquity of its own, giving the property an air of timelessness that Fanny Kemble would have admired.

SPOLETO FETE

Serves 6

Wine Cooler
Springtime Asparagus Soup
Salmon Roll-Ups
Chicken Teriyaki
Artichokes with Vinaigrette
Butter Bean Salad
Cream Cheese Wafers
Strawberries Unusual
Crisp Chocolate Chip Cookies

Wine Cooler

Yields 8 servings

1 fifth white wine
3¾ cups Sprite
1 apple, sliced
1 orange or kiwi, peeled and sliced

Pour wine and Sprite into pitcher. Chill. Add fruit and serve.

Springtime Asparagus Soup

Yields 5 cups

¼ cup (½ stick) butter or margarine
1 bunch green onions, chopped
2 pounds fresh asparagus
1 13¾-ounce can chicken broth
2 teaspoons lemon juice
¾ teaspoon salt
⅛ teaspoon pepper
½ cup light cream
Lemon slices for garnish

Melt butter in 3-quart saucepan. Add onions and sauté until tender. Snap off tough ends of asparagus and discard. Cut remaining stalks into 1-inch pieces. Add to onions. Add chicken broth, lemon juice, salt and pepper. Cook over medium heat 15 to 20 minutes or until asparagus is tender. Remove from heat. Transfer to blender and blend mixture until smooth. Return to original pan. Gradually add cream, stirring to blend. Serve immedi-ately for hot soup. Chill for several hours to serve cold. Garnish with sliced lemon.

Salmon Roll-Ups

Yields approximately 40

2 small onions
8 ounces cream cheese, softened
2 tablespoons half-and-half
¾ pound smoked salmon, sliced thin
2 3½-ounce jars capers, drained

In food processor, finely chop onions; add cream cheese and half-and-half; blend. Separate salmon slices; cut into rectangles, approximately 2 by 4 inches. Spread cream cheese mixture onto salmon. Sprinkle with capers. Beginning with large end, roll. Insert toothpick and place on serving platter. Chill at least 1 hour before serving. May halve recipe.

Chicken Teriyaki

Yields 6 servings

¼ cup soy sauce
2 tablespoons salad oil
1 teaspoon ground ginger
1 clove garlic, minced
1 2.6-ounce jar sesame seeds
4 whole chicken breasts, boned, or
*   2 pounds chicken nuggets*
18 6-inch skewers

Skin chicken breasts and cut into bite-sized nuggets. Place nuggets in shallow pan. Mix soy sauce, salad oil, ginger and garlic. Pour over chicken and marinate for at least 1 hour. If skewers are wooden, soak in water before using. Place 2 to 3 nuggets on skewer; cook on charcoal grill for 5 minutes per side or until tender. Pour sesame seeds on a cookie sheet; toast. Roll cooked chicken in seeds until coated.

Artichokes with Vinaigrette
Yields 6 servings

6 artichokes
1 lemon, halved
Salt to taste
Vinaigrette

Cut off stalks of artichokes, pull off tough leaves, and trim tips of remaining leaves with a pair of sharp scissors. Cut off about one-fourth of the top of the artichoke with a sharp knife. Choose a pan large enough to accommodate the artichokes. Fill with enough water to barely cover artichokes; squeeze the juice of a lemon into the water and toss in the rinds. Add salt to taste. Bring water to a boil. Add artichokes and cook 20 to 25 minutes until the base is tender. Remove artichokes from water and drain upside down on a rack. Artichokes may be served hot or cold. The "choke" in the center may be removed before serving by using a spoon to scrape out the dry, bristly portion, or this may be done at the table by the diner. To serve with Vinaigrette, provide a small cup of sauce, placed in center of artichoke or alongside.

VINAIGRETTE
Yields 1½ cups

¾ cup salad oil
⅓ cup tarragon vinegar
1 teaspoon salt
1 to 2 cloves garlic, minced
¼ cup minced sweet pickle
¼ cup minced parsley
¼ cup minced green pepper
¼ cup minced green onion

Combine ingredients in jar with tightly fitting lid. Shake well and refrigerate several hours before serving. Vinaigrette is also excellent on fried fish or shrimp.

Butter Bean Salad
Yields 6 servings

1 16-ounce bag frozen baby butter
   or lima beans
½ cup chopped celery
½ cup chopped green pepper
½ cup chopped green or red onion
½ cup mayonnaise
½ cup sour cream
1 teaspoon dry ranch dressing mix
Salt and pepper to taste
4 to 6 slices bacon, cooked and crumbled

Defrost beans in colander. Pat dry with paper towel. Mix beans, celery, green pepper and onion together. In separate bowl mix mayonnaise, sour cream, ranch dressing, salt and pepper. Combine the two mixtures and sprinkle with crumbled bacon. Chill and serve.

Cream Cheese Wafers

Yields 24 2-inch wafers

½ cup (1 stick) butter, melted
3 ounces cream cheese, softened
1 cup flour

Combine the above ingredients; dough will be very soft. Roll into a log 2 inches in diameter. Chill for several hours or overnight. Slice log into ½-inch-thick rounds and bake at 425° on an ungreased cookie sheet for about 10 minutes or until golden brown. This recipe may be doubled. Dough may be frozen before wafers are baked; cooked wafers may also be frozen. Hide these—they will disappear quickly!

Strawberries Unusual

Yields 6 servings

¼ cup (½ stick) butter
1 cup sugar
½ cup fresh orange juice
2 tablespoons Cointreau
1 quart strawberries, washed and capped

2 teaspoons coarsely ground black pepper
1 cup heavy cream
3 tablespoons confectioners' sugar
½ teaspoon vanilla extract

In a heavy skillet (iron is best), over moderate heat, melt the butter. Add the sugar and orange juice; cook mixture for 3 to 5 minutes until sugar is dissolved. Add the Cointreau and the strawberries, saving 6 to 12 for garnish; cook the mixture for 2 minutes—just until berries are heated. Add the pepper. In a chilled bowl, beat the cream until soft peaks form. Add the sugar and vanilla; beat until they are incorporated. To serve, divide the strawberry mixture into 6 long-stemmed glasses. Top each with whipped cream. Garnish with a strawberry.

Crisp Chocolate Chip Cookies

Yields 8 dozen

1 cup (2 sticks) butter or margarine,
    softened
1 cup vegetable oil
1 cup white granulated sugar
1 cup sifted confectioners' sugar
2 eggs, at room temperature
4 cups all-purpose flour
1 teaspoon baking soda
1 teaspoon cream of tartar
1 teaspoon salt
1 teaspoon vanilla extract

Continued . . .

12 ounces semisweet chocolate chips
¼ to ⅓ cup additional granulated sugar

Combine the first 5 ingredients in a large bowl and beat until smooth. Combine flour, soda, cream of tartar and salt; add to butter mixture and beat until smooth.

Stir in vanilla and chocolate chips. For each cookie, drop heaping teaspoon of mixture into a small bowl of granulated sugar to coat. Place balls 2 inches apart on ungreased cookie sheets. Bake at 375° for 10 to 12 minutes or until lightly browned. Cool cookies on wire rack.

FACING PAGE

Springtime Asparagus Soup and Salmon Roll-Ups await guests on the raised garden terrace of the William Gibbes house.

A buffet table featuring Breakfast Steak, Mepkin Abbey Incredible Eggs, Broiled Peach Halves and Fresh Melon Compote in the spacious hall of the Governor Thomas Bennett house.

House Party Brunch
The Governor Thomas Bennett House

T HE PROFITABLE rice and indigo plantations are abundant sources of wealth for many considerable families, who therefore give themselves to the enjoyment of every pleasure and convenience to which their warmer climate and better circumstances invite them," observed visiting German Johann Schopf in 1784. But rice fortunes were not confined to the planters alone. Governor Thomas Bennett, the builder of this spacious late Federal mansion, amassed a fortune as the owner of mills that processed both rice and lumber. The business had been started by his father, Thomas Bennett, Sr., who had bought large tracts of land in this early suburb of the city known as Harleston.

Powered by water from adjacent tidal creeks, Bennett's mills stood in close proximity to the house. His millpond was filled in about 1875 and for many years the site was occupied by the old Charleston Museum. An 1846 painting of Charleston by Henry Jackson, now in the collection of the Gibbes Museum of Art, shows the millpond and the vastly different landscape of the area before it was reclaimed and filled in like so much of the peninsular city.

Thomas Bennett, Sr., excelled as a lumberman, contractor and architect. In 1792, his design for the Charleston Orphan House was selected from those submitted. The need for such an institution had arisen due to the large number of children left parent-

The border above is from a design in the Governor Bennett house.

less by a series of yellow fever epidemics. It was a large brick building of four stories, roughcast, with a wooden cupola. Tragically, it fell victim to the wrecker's ball in 1953.

Bennett's son, Thomas Bennett, Jr., inherited his father's love of architecture. Serving as governor of South Carolina from 1820 to 1822, he completed his substantial town mansion in 1822 on land inherited from his father. A house of two and one-half stories set on a high English basement, it is one of the grandest and most beautiful dwellings in the city. A piazza of turned columns mounted with carved acanthus leaves over the capitals adorns the southern facade.

The interiors feature some of Charleston's most exuberant plaster decoration. Rich plaster cornices throughout the house incorporate anthemia, one of the principal motifs of classical ornament resembling the honeysuckle flower and leaf.

From the piazza one enters the hall by way of an elaborate doorway with delicately traced fanlight and sidelights. An arch frames the magnificent elliptical free-flying staircase, one of only two in the city. The other, slightly earlier example of this form is in the Nathaniel Russell house on Meeting Street.

Bennett's house was designed to impress. The staircase leads to an equally spectacular second-floor hall to the side of which is the primary reception room, an elaborately decorated drawing room with an imported gray-and-white marble mantel with Ionic columns and a carved panel depicting a basket of grapes.

In 1927, the Medical Society of South Carolina Trustees obtained the property for $11,000. It has been thoroughly restored and, under the auspices of the Roper Foundation, the house is frequently open for receptions when it resounds with the entertainments for which it was built.

COMING in from the sea . . . you have a fine prospect of the bay (which in some places is three miles broad) and of Charles Town at 9 or 10 miles distance, which lying open to the sea fronts you as you come in and makes a very handsome appearance, for it spreads a great deal of ground and there are in it several large capital good looking buildings, such as the royal exchange and custom house in one, which is a very substantial handsome large building of brick, faced with stone round the arches of the windows doors etc, also two very large handsome English churches that appear like stone buildings, and several spires belonging to different meeting houses, the Dutch and French churches etc etc. All of which being lofty present themselves to your view above the houses many miles off as you approach the town; but what adds greatly to the prospect coming in from the sea is Sulivan's Island at the mouth of the bay on the right hand, and Ashley and Coopers Rivers running up on each side the town. These, together with the appearance of the town itself, and a fine fertile looking country well wooded with noble lofty pines and oaks, for a prospect upon the whole strikingly beautiful.

"Charleston, S.C., in 1774 as Described by an English Traveller"

MACNAIR & MAXWELL
ON THE BAY

HYSON, green, gouchong, and bohea teas — coffie, double and fingle refined fugar, beft pearl barley, India fago, fhefhite and Glouchefter cheefe.

SPICERIES

Black pepper, nutmegs, cloves, cinamon, mace, trufles, morells, and vernicetti.

PICKLES

Oil, ketchup, anchovies, capers, mangoes, olives, girkins, walnuts, French beans, and excellent wine vinegar.

CONFECTIONARY

Currant jelly, Varverry comfits, fine Caraways, Scotch ditto, mixed comfits, capillaire and orgeat.

Also Beft Jamaica Spirits, and Weft India rum, cogniac and Britifh Brandy, Geneva, old Madeira xxx.

Royal Gazette
May 13, 1781

HOUSE PARTY BRUNCH

Serves 8

Sherry Cobbler
Fresh Melon Compote
Breakfast Steak
Mepkin Abbey Incredible Eggs
Broiled Peach Halves
Orange Glazed Rolls
Biscuits
Honey Jelly
Fig Preserves

Sherry Cobbler

Yields 1 serving

1½ ounces sherry
¼ cup pineapple juice
¼ cup cranberry juice
Chilled soda water
Mint sprig

Mix sherry and juices; pour over ice in a tall tumbler. Top off glass with soda water and add a sprig of mint.

Fresh Melon Compote

Yields 8 servings

2 cups cantaloupe balls
2 cups honeydew melon balls
2 cups watermelon balls
½ cup fresh blueberries
2 tablespoons lime juice
Mint leaves

Combine fruits in large bowl. Sprinkle lime juice over fruits, mixing gently. Serve in sherbet glasses and garnish with mint leaves.

Breakfast Steak

Yields 8 servings

4 English muffins, split
6 tablespoons butter, divided
8 small beef tenderloins, ½ inch thick

3 to 4 tablespoons Worcestershire sauce
2 medium tomatoes
4 tablespoons tarragon vinegar

Spread muffin halves with butter and toast until lightly browned. Sauté steaks in remaining butter, laced with Worcestershire sauce, until done to taste. Remove to platter and keep warm. Cut tomatoes into eight slices, ½ inch thick; brown the slices in pan drippings. Place one tomato slice on each muffin half and top with a steak. Add vinegar to pan; heat, scraping pan to loosen drippings. Pour over steaks before serving.

Mepkin Abbey Incredible Eggs

Yields 8 servings

2 tablespoons butter
½ cup chopped onion
½ cup chopped green pepper
8 eggs
¼ cup milk
1 teaspoon seasoned salt
½ teaspoon crushed dried basil
¼ teaspoon black pepper
3 ounces cream cheese, cubed
1 medium tomato, chopped
2 to 4 slices bacon, cooked and crumbled

In a large skillet over medium heat, cook onion and green pepper in butter until tender. Mix eggs, milk and seasonings; pour over onions and green pepper. Add

cheese and tomato. Gently push spatula completely across bottom and sides of skillet, forming large soft curds. Cook until eggs are thickened throughout but still moist. Sprinkle with bacon. Serve immediately.

Broiled Peach Halves
Yields 8 servings

8 fresh peaches, freestone if possible
¼ cup (½ stick) butter
4 teaspoons brown sugar

Peel peaches; halve and remove pits. Place on baking sheet, cut side up. Dot with butter and sprinkle with brown sugar. Broil until bubbly and lightly browned.

Orange Glazed Rolls
Yields 18 rolls

1 package dry yeast
¼ cup warm water
1 cup sugar, divided
1 teaspoon salt
2 eggs
½ cup sour cream
½ cup (1 stick) butter, melted and divided
3½ cups flour
2 tablespoons grated orange rind
Orange Glaze

Dissolve yeast in warm water; let stand for 10 minutes. Beat together ¼ cup sugar, salt, eggs, sour cream and 6 table- spoons melted butter until thoroughly combined. Add yeast mixture. Gradually add 2 cups flour; beat until smooth and elastic. Add remaining flour to mixture. Knead. Let rise until doubled in size, about 2 hours. Roll dough into two 12- by-8-inch rectangles, ¼ to ½ inch thick. Combine ¾ cup sugar and orange rind. Brush each rectangle with 1 tablespoon of melted butter and spread with half of orange-sugar mixture. Roll up, starting with wide end. Cut each into 9 rolls. Place in greased 9-by-13-inch pan. Cover and let rise one hour or until doubled in bulk. Bake at 350° for 25 minutes until golden brown. Pour Orange Glaze over warm rolls as soon as they are removed from the oven.

ORANGE GLAZE

¾ cup sugar
½ cup sour cream
2 tablespoons orange juice
½ cup (1 stick) butter

In a medium saucepan over medium heat, combine all ingredients. Bring to a boil. Boil for 5 minutes.

Biscuits
Yields 24 2-inch biscuits

2¼ cups self-rising flour
½ cup (1 stick) butter, thoroughly chilled
¾ cup milk
1 teaspoon sugar

Continued . . .

Place flour and butter in food processor and blend until mixture is the consistency of coarse corn meal. With processor running, add milk and sugar and blend until dough ball is formed. Turn onto a lightly floured surface and roll dough ¼ to ½ inch thick. Cut into rounds 1½ inches thick. Place on an ungreased baking sheet and bake at 450° for 12 to 15 minutes or until brown.

Honey Jelly
Yields 2 pints

2½ cups honey
½ cup light corn syrup
¾ cup water
3 tablespoons lemon juice
3 ounces liquid pectin (1 pouch)

In a large pot (not aluminum or enamel), stir together the honey, corn syrup, water and lemon juice. Over medium heat, bring to a boil. Boil vigorously for 1 to 2 minutes. Stir in pectin. Return mixture to a rolling boil that cannot be stirred down. Boil for exactly 1 minute. Remove from heat and set aside for 1 minute or until the foam comes to the top. Quickly skim off the foam and pour into hot sterilized jars. Leave ¼ to ½ inch head-space. Seal.

Fig Preserves
Yields 6 half-pints

4 pounds figs, unpeeled
1 cup water
4 cups sugar
Juice of 1 lemon

In a Dutch oven, simmer the figs in water until soft. Mash figs; add sugar and lemon juice. Simmer until mixture reaches the thickness of medium white sauce. Put preserves in hot sterilized jars, seal and process in water bath for 5 minutes.

Lowcountry Seafood Dinner
Mount Pleasant

JUST ACROSS the Cooper River from Charleston is the peaceful village of Mount Pleasant. Bounded by Charleston Harbor, Shem Creek and Cove Inlet, the area was initially settled in 1680 when Florentia O'Sullivan, a surveyor general of the colony, was granted 2,340 acres of land. This grant included the barrier island, Sullivan's, which still bears his name, and a portion of the neck of land that would eventually become Mount Pleasant.

In the eighteenth century, this area consisted of several hamlets: Greenwich, Hilliardsville, Lucasville, Hibben's Ferry and Mount Pleasant, the last being a plantation tract owned by Jacob Motte. In the nineteenth century, as these hamlets merged, the area took the name Mount Pleasant.

Before the Grace Memorial Bridge was opened in 1929, access to Mount Pleasant from Charleston was provided by a variety of ferry services. During his 1791 visit, President George Washington arrived in Charleston on a barge manned by twelve oarsmen. On March 12, 1840, this advertisement appeared in the *Charleston Courier:*

MOUNT PLEASANT VILLAGE — SUMMER RETREAT

The undersigned, having leased the Ferry known as Hibben's, is now prepared to convey Passengers to and fro from the City. Hours of

starting, viz.: Leaves the Ferry 8 A.M. and 3 P.M.: leaves Ferry slip, foot of Queen St., 11 A.M. and 5 P.M. Persons can be accommodated with board by the day or week at the Ferry House, at a reasonable rate. Parties wishing to spend the day can have the boats at any hour by sending word the day previous. Horses, stabled and every attention paid to them. — Thomas Quinby

N.B. Families can be supplied with groceries and Dry Goods at Town prices at the store attached to the Ferry House.

The old village of Mount Pleasant retains much of its early charm with ancient live oaks framing beautiful views and vistas. Its picturesque nature was recognized even in the mid-nineteenth century. Promoting the tranquil qualities of the town, a letter in the *Charleston Daily Courier* of August 15, 1858, included this description, which remains true in part:

> I cannot say that there is any great room here for the descriptive powers except such as our beautiful groves and woodlands afford to the eye of the lover of the beautiful in nature. . . . We have no very elegant specimens of architecture to boast of. Our houses were built in the good old times, when the march of improvement had not laid its vandal hand on the simple forest beauties, which constitute the chief glory of a place like this, and people were satisfied with the plain one story cottages, usually inhabited by farmers and planters as temporary retreats from the impure air of their country estates. . . .

One of the most beautiful spots in the village is this point overlooking pleasure-boat docks and the skyline of Charleston in the distance. The house is called "O Be Joyful," an appropriate place for a celebration of Lowcountry seafood on the lawn.

LOWCOUNTRY SEAFOOD DINNER

Serves 8

Chuck's Martini
Annie's Skewered Scallops
Charlotte's Clams
Nancy's She-Crab Soup
Baked Tuna Fillets or Nelson's Fried Fish
with Green Peppercorn Sauce
King Street Shrimp
Stuffed Squash • Tomato Pie
Strawberry and Fig Salad
Corn Sticks
Peaches in Brioche

Chuck's Martini

Yields 1 serving

2 ounces gin or vodka
½ ounce dry vermouth
Drop of Scotch
3 cocktail onions

Mix gin or vodka and vermouth in a shaker of ice; drain into frosted glass; add a small drop of Scotch. Serve with cocktail onions on a toothpick.

Annie's
Skewered Scallops

Yields 8 to 10 servings

½ cup olive oil
2 tablespoons fresh lemon juice
2 teaspoons lemon pepper
½ teaspoon minced garlic
1 pound small bay scallops
8 slices very lean bacon, sliced very thin

Combine the oil, lemon juice, lemon pepper and minced garlic. Add scallops and marinate for several hours. Cut each slice of bacon into thirds. Wrap the bacon around the scallops and skewer. Grill or broil in oven for 4 minutes on each side, being careful not to burn bacon or overcook scallops.

Charlotte's Clams

Yields 8 servings

24 small clams in shell
3 cups rock salt
6 strips bacon, cut into fourths
½ cup grated Cheddar cheese

Immediately after harvesting clams, place in a plastic bag in the freezer. They may be stored there for up to 2 weeks. Remove from freezer and shells will pop open. Discard top shell and arrange clams on a bed of rock salt in a 9-by-13-inch pan. Cover each clam with a quarter piece of bacon and a teaspoon of grated cheese. Broil for about 5 minutes and serve hot with a cocktail fork.

Nancy's
She-Crab Soup

Yields 8 servings

¼ cup (½ stick) butter
3 tablespoons finely chopped onion
½ teaspoon paprika
Dash Accent
4 tablespoons flour
4 cups milk, heated
½ pound fresh crab meat, more if desired
1½ ounces crab roe or yolks of
*   2 hard-cooked eggs*

Salt and freshly ground pepper to taste
2 tablespoons dry sherry

In top of double boiler, melt butter. Add onion, cooking until transparent. Add seasonings and flour. Stir to make a roux. Add hot milk, stirring with a wire whisk. Simmer for 3 minutes. Add crab meat, crab roe, salt and pepper, and sherry. Simmer on low heat for 20 minutes. Serve immediately.

Baked
Tuna Fillets

Yields 8 servings

8 tuna fillets
1½ cups sour cream
1 bunch green onions, chopped
2 tablespoons capers
1 tablespoon mayonnaise
1 teaspoon lemon juice
¼ cup Parmesan cheese

Place fillets in a buttered baking dish. Mix together the sour cream, onions, capers, mayonnaise and lemon juice. Cover fillets with sour cream mixture. Bake at 350° for 20 minutes or until fish tests done. Sprinkle Parmesan cheese over all and return to broiler until lightly browned.

Nelson's Fried Fish
with Green Peppercorn
Sauce

Yields 6 to 8 servings

6 to 8 large fish fillets
1 to 2 eggs
2 tablespoons water
1½ to 2 cups biscuit mix
½ teaspoon freshly ground pepper
Peanut oil for frying
Green Peppercorn Sauce

Pat fish dry; set aside. Mix together eggs and water until thoroughly blended; set aside. In another flat pan, mix together biscuit mix and pepper; set aside. In assembly-line style, dip fish in egg wash, then in biscuit mixture. Thoroughly coat each piece of fish, placing on a platter. Continue until all fillets are thoroughly coated. In a large, heavy frying pan, add ½ to 1 inch of oil. When oil is hot (not smoking), carefully add each fillet. Cook until golden-brown on each side. Using a slotted pancake turner, carefully remove from heat; place on heated platter. Place in 250° oven until ready to serve. Serve with Green Peppercorn Sauce.

GREEN PEPPERCORN SAUCE
  Yields 1½ cups

1 2-ounce jar green peppercorns, drained
2 teaspoons beef or chicken bouillon granules

Continued . . .

½ cup dry white wine
2 teaspoons dried thyme or tarragon
1 cup heavy cream
2 tablespoons brandy
2 tablespoons butter

In a 1-quart saucepan, combine all ingredients except butter. Simmer over low heat until mixture is slightly reduced. While cooking, whisk in 1 teaspoon of butter at a time. Do not allow to boil. If sauce is too thin, thicken over low heat by adding a little cornstarch (1 teaspoon dissolved in 2 tablespoons of water). If sauce should separate, try beating in a little ice water. Serve immediately.

King Street Shrimp

Yields 8 to 10 servings

½ cup chopped celery
½ cup chopped bell pepper
1 large onion, chopped
¼ cup (½ stick) butter
2 cups cooked rice
2 pounds shrimp, boiled, peeled and deveined
1 can tomato soup
1 tablespoon Worcestershire sauce
1 8-ounce jar medium sliced mushrooms, drained
½ pound sharp Cheddar cheese, grated and divided in half

Sauté celery, bell pepper and onion in butter. Mix with remaining ingredients, excluding half of the cheese. Place mixture in a 9-by-13-inch casserole dish; sprinkle remaining cheese on top. Bake at 350° for ½ hour.

Stuffed Squash

Yields 8 servings

8 medium yellow squash
1 cup chopped spring onions, including green tops
1 large tomato, chopped
1 cup shredded Monterey Jack cheese
4 slices bacon, cooked and crumbled
Salt and pepper to taste
1 cup bread crumbs
2 to 3 tablespoons butter, melted

Wash squash; cover with water and bring to a boil. Simmer 10 minutes, or until tender but still firm. Drain and cool. Halve each squash and scoop out center pulp, leaving a thin shell. Combine pulp with onions, tomato, cheese and bacon. Fill squash shells with the pulp mixture. Sprinkle each with bread crumbs and one teaspoon of butter. Place in two 9-by-12-inch baking dishes. Bake at 400° for 20 minutes.

Tomato Pie*
Yields 8 to 10 servings

3 tomatoes, sliced thin
1 can butterflake biscuits
1 cup chopped celery
1 cup chopped onion
½ cup chopped bell pepper
1 tablespoon butter
1 teaspoon Mrs. Dash
1 cup grated mild Cheddar cheese

Press biscuits into bottom of ungreased 9-by-12-inch pan. Place sliced tomatoes on top. Sauté other vegetables in butter until transparent but still crisp; drain on paper towel. Cover tomatoes evenly with vegetable mixture. Sprinkle with Mrs. Dash and cheese.

TOPPING
1 cup low-calorie mayonnaise
1 cup sour cream

Mix together ingredients. Cover cheese with mixture and seal to edges. Bake at 350° for 45 minutes until top is golden brown and bubbly around edges. Allow to stand 15 to 20 minutes before slicing.

Courtesy Gateway Magazine.

Strawberry and Fig Salad
Yields 8 servings

2 teaspoons balsamic vinegar
2 tablespoons shredded fresh basil leaves
2 pints halved strawberries
6 fresh figs, quartered
Lettuce leaves

Combine vinegar and basil in a small bowl. Add fruit and toss. Serve on lettuce leaves.

Corn Sticks
Yields 12 to 14 sticks

2 eggs
1½ cups buttermilk
1 teaspoon salt
¼ teaspoon baking soda
1½ cups white corn meal
½ cup flour
½ cup butter, melted

In bowl, beat together eggs and buttermilk; add salt and baking soda. Stir in corn meal and flour. Add butter. Pour batter into 2 greased, hot corn stick pans. (Some like to use bacon fat to coat the pans.) Bake at 425° for 20 minutes or until golden brown.

Peaches in Brioche

Yields 8 servings

8 small fresh peaches
1 cup sugar
¾ cup water
¼ teaspoon ground ginger
¼ teaspoon cardamom
2 tablespoons Amaretto
2 tablespoons brandy
8 brioche rolls
3 tablespoons butter, softened

Peel and halve peaches; remove pits. Bring sugar and water to a boil. Add ginger, cardamom and peaches. Simmer for 15 minutes, uncovered. Add Amaretto and brandy and continue cooking for 5 to 10 minutes until peaches are tender. Remove peaches with slotted spoon and reduce syrup by one-third over medium heat. Pour syrup over peach halves and refrigerate. Remove tops of brioches and scoop out all but thin shell. Spread with butter and bake in 350° oven for 10 to 15 minutes, until crisp. Place 2 peach halves in each brioche shell, replace top and drizzle with syrup. Serve with a dollop of whipped cream, if desired.

FACING PAGE

As the sun sets over Charleston Harbor, a seafood buffet including King Street Shrimp, Nancy's She-Crab Soup and Baked Tuna Fillets is served.

*Marinated Pork Tenderloin,
Grilled Tomatoes and
Corn on the Cob.*

*Marsha's Salsa with
Tortilla Chips.*

*The shaded kitchen garden of the James Vanderhorst house
is readied for a summertime cookout buffet.*

*Flower Pot Sundaes
with Hot Fudge Sauce.*

Summer Cookout
The James Vanderhorst House

SUMMERTIME in Charleston, a season immortalized in Gershwin's opera *Porgy and Bess*: Not everyone found the living easy, however. One early chronicler found Charleston to be a heaven in the spring, a hell in the summer, and a hospital in the fall. The low-lying situation of Charleston and environs had its benefits, to be sure, but there were also drawbacks. Eliza Lucas Pinckney, who worked diligently to promote the cultivation of indigo, wrote to her brother Thomas in 1742: "The winters here are very fine and pleasant, but 4 months in the year is extremely disagreeable, excessive hott, much thunder and lightening, and muskatoes and sand flies in abundance."

"Muskatoes" were no help in controlling the various outbreaks of malaria which plagued the early city. In an effort to protect the occupants, the practice of using gauze mosquito netting or "pavilions" on bedsteads arose. The well-known naturalist John Bartram commented on the situation during his visit in August 1765. If his spelling and punctuation are somewhat archaic, his meaning is quite clear:

> . . . in Charleston all good livers has what they call muschata curtains or
> pavilions some is silk some linen silk grass or Gaws thay are wove on
> purpose for that use & make a very comfortable lodging amongst
> thousands of those hungry vermin that infested all thair lodgings I
> thought at first that they would be stifling hot but upon tryall I found

them very pleasant as thay are fine & so thin wove Just to keep out ye fly but if they have any hole in big enough to put ones little finder end int thay will fint it & torment us all by piercing our skin before morning if we arc uncovered which is not uncommon in hot weather . . .

Such impediments to the enjoyment of Carolina summers prompted something of a mini evacuation during the middle months of the year as early as the 1730's when Newport, Rhode Island, emerged as a favorite destination for vacationing wealthy Charlestonians. In the nineteenth century, the airy, mountainous region of western North Carolina provided relief and Flat Rock became (and still is) the favorite retreat for Charlestonians seeking shelter from hot and humid Lowcountry summers.

The conveniences of later twentieth-century life now allow the advantages of summer to outweigh the perils. Summer entertaining takes the form of informal outdoor gatherings like this cookout in the garden of the pre-Revolutionary James Vanderhorst house. Located on Tradd Street, one of the city's earliest and most architecturally intact, it is a picturesque building with a handsome balcony added over the high entrance in 1927 by Charleston artist Alfred Hutty and Mrs. Hutty. Based in Woodstock, New York, the Huttys spent thirty-five winters in Charleston and carried out the initial restoration on their property, converting the original separate kitchen building into Mr. Hutty's studio. There he produced many of his delightful etchings and paintings of Charleston scenes which remain sought-after collector's items today. Garden walls of old Charleston brick enclose the property and provide a pleasant backdrop for outdoor entertaining.

. . . [E]ven the sandy soil about Charles Town is naturally very fertile, but that I take to be chiefly owing to the favorableness of the climate 7 months in the year being certainly very fine, pleasant, healthy and temperate, for in the severest winters there is never above 8 or 10 days frost at the most, and in general not above 5 or 6. The greatest part of the other 5 months is a very disagreeable relaxing heat, subject at the end of the year to bad fall fevers. The thermomiter I am told was once last year as high as 98, but those extreem heats don't last long, the changes from them to quite cool weather being very sudden, owing to violent storms of heavy rain and very severe thunder and lightening which tho' common in Charles Town seldom does any mischief for almost every house has one conductor and some two by which prudent precaution I dare say they are often preserved from terrible accidents that would otherwise most probably frequently happen from the lightening, which is uncommonly sharp and dreadful to behold.

"Charleston, S.C., in 1774 as Described by an English Traveller"

SICILY WINE, &c.

JUST RECEIVED AND FOR SALE, BY
LEDUC & DANJOU,
CORNER OF CHURCH AND TRADD STREETS,

Fifteen pipes of old Sicily Wine, nearly equal to Madeira
London bottled Brown Stout
A few pipes of clear white Bordeaux Brandy, fit to make
Ratafie, &c.
Orange Shrub of a fuperior quality
A few tierces of white wine Pickling Vinegar
White and Green Wax Candles, in fmall boxes.

— ALSO —

Conftantly on hand, and may be procured by any quantity
at the above place, and on accommodating terms,

THE FOLLOWING ARTICLES, viz:

Beft L.P. Madeira, Sherry, Lifbon, Port, Teneriffe,
Malaga, Champaigne, Frontignac, Vin-de-Grave, and
Claret Wines, of the moft approved kinds

Old Cognac Brandy; old and mellow Jamaica Spirits and
other Rum; real Holland and Country Gin; Rafpberry and
Cherry Brandy; Marginique Cordials of almoft every
defcriptions; Stoughton's Bitters; frefh Teas of different
kinds; Loaf, Lump, and Brown Sugar; Coffee and
Chocalate; Fruit, preserved in Brandy; afforted Pickles;
Spices of all kinds; Spanifh Cigarrs; Spermaceti and
Tallow Candles; clear Soap in fmall boxes fit for family ufe;
Sallad, Paints, and Spermaceti Oil; with every other Article
in the Grocery Line.

The Times, Charleston
April 22, 1808

SUMMER COOKOUT

Serves 6

Heyward's Market Margaritas
Marsha's Salsa with Tortilla Chips
Cold Black Bean Soup
Marinated Pork Tenderloin
Grilled Tomatoes
Grilled Corn on the Cob
Skewered Vegetables
French Bread
Flower Pot Sundaes with Hot Fudge Sauce

Heyward's
Market Margaritas
Yields 6 servings

3 large limes
6 tablespoons water
9 ounces Triple Sec
9 ounces tequila
Coarse salt

Chill 8-ounce glasses. Squeeze limes and pour juice into container. Add water, tequila and Triple Sec. May be stored in the refrigerator at this point. Before serving, moisten rims of glasses and dip in coarse salt. Pour tequila mixture into glasses and add ice. May divide recipe by 6 for 1 serving.

Marsha's Salsa
Yields 5 cups

1 cup coarsely chopped fresh cilantro, or
  coriander or Chinese parsley leaves
4 cups coarsely chopped tomatoes, drained
1 cup chopped red onion
1 tablespoon white vinegar
1 tablespoon salad oil
Salt and pepper to taste

Mix all ingredients and serve with tortilla chips. Delicious substitute for taco sauce. This is a mild sauce; if you prefer medium to hot, add hot pepper sauce to taste.

Cold
Black Bean Soup
Yields 8 to 10 servings

2 cups black beans
2 quarts cold water
1 ham hock or ham bone and meat
2 to 3 cups chopped onion
2 cloves garlic, minced
4 tablespoons chopped fresh parsley
½ teaspoon salt
½ teaspoon freshly ground pepper
Dash Tabasco
⅓ cup red wine or sherry, optional
2 tablespoons lemon juice
½ cup sour cream
2 tomatoes, chopped
4 tablespoons chopped parsley
2 tablespoons chopped green onion

Cover beans with water and soak overnight. Drain. Fill soup pot with 8 cups cold water, beans and ham hock. Cook on low heat until tender—about 3 hours. Add onions, garlic and parsley; add seasonings and wine. Continue cooking over low heat for one more hour or until beans are desired tenderness. Chill. Skim off fat. Stir in lemon juice. Serve with a dollop of sour cream in center of bowl encircled by a ring of chopped tomatoes, parsley and onion. Salsa may be substituted for the vegetables, if desired.

Marinated Pork Tenderloin
Yields 6 servings

1 2½-pound pork tenderloin
½ cup brown sugar
½ cup Dijon mustard
¼ cup bourbon
¼ cup soy sauce
1 garlic clove, minced
2 teaspoons Worcestershire sauce
Salt and pepper to taste

Tie tenderloin with string at 1-inch intervals. To make marinade, blend together sugar, mustard, bourbon, soy sauce, garlic, Worcestershire, salt and pepper. Marinate pork for 12 hours. Cook on grill, closing cover, for 45 minutes to 1 hour, being sure to rotate.

Grilled Tomatoes
Yields 6 servings

6 tomatoes
Salt and pepper
2 tablespoons margarine, melted
1 tablespoon Parmesan cheese

Cut tomatoes into 6 wedges, leaving stem ends intact. Carefully spread wedges apart; salt and pepper the inside; coat with margarine. Sprinkle with ½ tea-spoon of Parmesan cheese. Wrap each tomato in aluminum foil and cook on grill 10 to 15 minutes or until tender.

Grilled Corn on the Cob
Yields 8 ears

1 quart water
3 tablespoons sugar
8 ears of corn
½ cup (1 stick) butter, melted
Seasoned salt or table salt

Peel back husk of corn, remove silk; wrap husk around corn. In shallow roasting pan, combine water and sugar. Add ears of corn and soak for 15 to 20 minutes. Remove corn from water. Wrap in aluminum foil, twisting ends to close. Place wrapped corn on grill 5 inches from heat. Roast for 15 to 20 minutes, turning often. To serve, use protective gloves and remove foil and husks. Place butter in shallow platter; roll corn in butter and then in seasoned salt. Serve quickly.

Skewered Vegetables
Yields 6 servings

½ cup vegetable oil
¼ cup lemon juice

Continued . . .

¼ cup vinegar
2 teaspoons Worcestershire sauce
2 teaspoons Italian seasoning
1 teaspoon salt
½ teaspoon pepper
2 green peppers, cut into ½-inch strips
2 zucchini, cut into ½-inch slices
12 whole mushrooms
12 small whole onions or 1 large onion
  cut into sections
12 6-inch skewers

In a gallon storage bag, combine vegetable oil, lemon juice, vinegar, Worcestershire sauce and seasonings, mixing well. Add vegetables, seal bag, and shake to distribute the marinade. Refrigerate 1 or more hours. Thread the vegetables onto 6-inch skewers (which have been soaked in water, if wooden). Grill over medium hot coals 10 to 15 minutes, turning and brushing occasionally with the marinade.

French Bread

Yields 2 loaves

1 package dry yeast
1 tablespoon sugar
1¼ cups water
1 teaspoon salt
4 to 4⅓ cups flour
1 egg white
1 tablespoon cold water

In small bowl, combine yeast with sugar and ¼ cup water. In larger bowl, add 1 cup water, salt, flour and yeast mixture. Mix until dough is sticky. Transfer to lightly floured board. Knead until dough is no longer sticky—approximately 10 minutes. Place dough in oiled bowl; cover with damp cloth. Let rise for 1½ to 2 hours or until doubled in bulk. Punch down; let rest 10 minutes. Transfer to floured bowl. Cut dough in half. Shape into two 18-inch loaves. Place in lightly oiled long loaf pan or on oiled cookie sheets. Cut 3 or 4 slashes in top of each loaf.

Let dough rise for 1 hour, or until doubled in bulk. Mix together egg white and 1 tablespoon of cold water. Using a pastry brush, gently coat dough with egg white mixture. Bake at 350° for 25 minutes or until brown and hollow-sounding when thumped. Let cool on wire racks. Slice and serve.

Flower Pot Sundaes

Yields 6 servings

6 chocolate wafers
6 clay flower pots, 3 inches in diameter
1 gallon ice cream
Hot Fudge Sauce

Wash flower pots; line bottom of each pot with a wafer. Place two large scoops of ice cream in each pot. Freeze. Right before

serving, drizzle Hot Fudge Sauce over ice cream. Garnish with toppings of your choice.

Hot Fudge Sauce
Yields 1 cup

½ cup heavy cream
3 tablespoons butter
⅓ cup sugar
⅓ cup dark brown sugar, packed
½ cup cocoa

In a heavy saucepan, combine all ingredients. Bring to a boil; remove from heat; refrigerate until ready to serve. To serve, heat for 30 seconds in a microwave, or heat slowly in heavy saucepan over low to medium flame. Sauce will keep for several weeks.

NOW LANDING,

From on board the Schooner Polly, juſt arrived from Philadelphia, at Champney's wharf,

AND FOR SALE,

Freſh butter in ſmall tubs
Northern Gin in barrels
Brown Soap, of an excellent quality, in boxes
Mould and dipped Candles, aſſorted, in boxes
Butter in kegs
Cyder, Apples, and Pears, in barrels.

Charleston Courier
February 12, 1804

Sunset Cruise
The Ashley and Cooper Rivers

D R. George Milligen-Johnston, writing in 1770, observed, "Charles-town is the Metropolis . . . Bay-Street which fronts Cooper-River and the Ocean, is really handsome, and must delight the Stranger who approacheth it from the sea." Charleston still delights the seafarer as it has for centuries. Arriving in 1773, visiting Bostonian Josiah Quincy noted in his diary,

> The number of shipping far surpassed all I had ever seen in Boston. I was told there were then not as many as common at this season, tho about 350 sail lay off the town. The town struck me very agreeably; but the New Exchange which fronted the place of my landing made a most noble appearance. The numbers of inhabitants and appearance of the buildings far exceeded my expectation.

The Exchange Building to which Quincy referred had been completed in 1771 to a design by William Rigby Naylor, a draftsman and purveyor of building materials. With its rusticated ground story, Venetian windows, cupola and ornamental stone urns, it must have had a commanding presence on the waterfront. Later infill and buildings have today obscured its preeminence on the Cooper River.

One hundred and one years before the completion of the Exchange, Carolina's first settlers had arrived in what is now Charleston Harbor and proceeded up the Ashley River to Albemarle Point, the site of the first settlement. Some 150 colonists made up the initial group sent to settle Carolina, the vast territory south of Virginia and north of Spanish Florida which had been granted by Charles II to eight political supporters. These Lords Proprietors were well-connected politicians and men of affairs who looked upon the landed estates of the New World as extra sources of income.

While not the recognized head of the Proprietors, Anthony Ashley Cooper, created Earl of Shaftesbury in 1672, soon emerged as the most influential of the group. An able and crafty politician, he managed to serve both Oliver Cromwell and Charles II and was appointed lord chancellor under the latter. Cooper's interest in colonial affairs extended to Barbados, where he had once owned a plantation. He had also invested heavily in the slave trade. His most lasting contribution to Carolina was the blueprint for its governance known as the Fundamental Constitutions of 1669, a document written by John Locke, a secretary to the Proprietors and to Cooper himself.

Under the Fundamental Constitutions, the distribution of lands and political authority were outlined in an attempt to create an orderly basis for society. The clauses governing religious toleration were particularly progressive for their time. Locke's document guaranteed religious freedom to the Indians ("ye natives . . . utterly strangers to Christianity, whose idolatry, ignorance, or mistake gives us noe right to expell or use ym. ill") and also to "yt. heathens, Jues, and other dissenters." The Anglican church was established and supported by taxes but no one was forced to belong to it. Thus, Charleston would become a haven for a great variety of settlers including Quakers, Presbyterians, Jews, Baptists, Huguenots and Methodists.

In 1680, the main settlement of Charles Town was moved to its present location on higher ground at the end of the peninsula bounded by the Ashley and Cooper rivers. Three years later, Anthony Ashley Cooper, Earl of Shaftesbury, died in Holland, exiled for attempting to exclude Charles's Catholic brother James from the line of succession. Soon, the rivers named for him would be dotted with wharves and sailing vessels of all types as Charleston emerged as a leading trading center.

CHARLES TOWN . . . is open to a fine, deep salt water bay in front or to the eastward, and to two very fine navigable rivers that run up from out of the bay on each side of the town, the first of which called Cooper's River inclines to the N.N.W. and runs navigable for large ships many miles into the country and vessels of 100 tons may go above 40 miles up it very safely. The other called Ashley River is a very fine one, where large ships can go several miles up and vessels of upwards of 100 tons may go above 20 miles up very well. Many fine ships are built up this river from 3 to 400 tons burthen and much cheaper than in England, for the whole province of South Carolina (before it is cultivated) naturally produces live oak, (which is rather harder and more durable than any English oak is) and several other different sorts of very good oaks, cedars, pitch pines and cyprus trees, also white and yellow pines in vast abundance, as fine and useful as any in the world, which are very fit for making good lower masts for any of the navy of England.

"Charleston, S.C., in 1774 as Described by an English Traveller"

SUNSET CRUISE

Serves 4

Modern Lemonade
Charleston Cheese Spread
Boiled Peanuts
Frosty Summer Soup
Shrimp Boats
Roast Beef Pockets
Tomatoes with Lime Dressing
Chilled Cucumbers
Lowcountry Figs
Brandy Snaps

Modern Lemonade

Yields 1 serving

1½ ounces dry sherry (not cream sherry)
1½ ounces sloe gin
1 to 1½ tablespoons sugar, extra fine
1 to 2 ounces lemon juice
Soda water

Mix in a shaker the sherry, sloe gin, sugar and lemon juice. Shake until sugar is dissolved. Fill 10- to 12-ounce glass with ice cubes. Pour mixture in glass; add soda water. Stir.

Charleston Cheese Spread

Yields 2 cups

8 ounces Gouda cheese
2 ounces blue cheese, crumbled
½ cup sour cream
¼ cup (½ stick) butter
2 tablespoons wine vinegar
1 tablespoon grated onion
Dash cayenne pepper

Peel the rind from Gouda cheese and shred cheese into a saucepan. Add all other ingredients, heating slowly. Stir constantly with whisk until cheeses are melted. Lightly oil a 2-cup mold; pour in cheese mixture. Cover and chill overnight. When ready to serve, unmold onto a serving plate. Garnish. Serve at room temperature with plain crackers.

Boiled Peanuts

Yields 5 servings

1 quart green peanuts
½ cup salt
2 quarts water

Wash peanuts thoroughly. Put peanuts in a large pot, cover with water and add salt. Bring water to a boil and simmer for 2 to 3 hours or until soft. Be sure to check on water and add more if necessary. Leave peanuts in water for another hour after cooking. Drain and serve. Peanuts keep well in refrigerator.

Frosty Summer Soup

Yields 4 to 6 servings

1 small onion, peeled and chopped
1 small cucumber, peeled and chopped
8 sprigs parsley
1 cup yogurt or sour cream
1 10¾-ounce can condensed tomato soup
1 10¾-ounce can chicken broth

In blender, puree onion, cucumber and parsley. Blend in yogurt or sour cream and tomato soup. Skim fat from broth and blend broth with other ingredients. Chill.

Shrimp Boats

Yields 4 servings

4 cucumbers of equal size
1 pound shrimp, boiled, peeled and deveined

Slice of carrot
Cocktail Sauce

½ teaspoon seasoned pepper
Crisp lettuce leaves

See instructions for making Shrimp Boats on page 194. Serve with individual containers of Cocktail Sauce.

Split pita pockets and set aside. Combine roast beef, celery, onion, pickle and capers; set aside. Blend together salad oil, vinegar, mustard, garlic salt and pepper. Toss roast beef mixture with dressing. Chill for at least one hour. Line pita pockets with lettuce, fill with beef mixture and serve.

Cocktail Sauce
Yields 1 cup

1 cup ketchup
1 teaspoon Worcestershire sauce
1 teaspoon horseradish
2 teaspoons lemon juice
⅛ teaspoon onion juice

Mix together ketchup, Worcestershire sauce, horseradish, lemon juice and onion juice. Chill before serving. May be kept in the refrigerator.

Tomatoes with Lime Dressing
Yields 4 servings

½ cup lime juice (approximately 3 limes)
¼ cup salad oil
½ teaspoon salt
½ teaspoon pepper
2 teaspoons brown sugar
4 tomatoes, sliced

Mix first five ingredients together and pour over tomatoes in a shallow bowl. Chill before serving.

Roast Beef Pockets
Yields 8 sandwiches

4 medium pita pockets
1 pound deli roast beef, sliced thin and julienned
½ cup chopped celery
4 tablespoons green onion, chopped
½ cup chopped dill pickle
2 tablespoons capers
½ cup salad oil
3 tablespoons vinegar
1 tablespoon Dijon mustard
½ teaspoon garlic salt

Chilled Cucumbers
Yields 4 servings

2 cucumbers
2 small purple onions
1 tablespoon olive oil
½ teaspoon garlic salt
½ pint sour cream
2 tablespoons lemon juice

Continued . . .

1 teaspoon sugar
½ teaspoon salt
¼ teaspoon freshly ground pepper

Peel and slice cucumbers and onions. Mix them gently in a deep bowl. Combine remaining ingredients and beat until smooth. Pour over sliced vegetables and chill for at least one hour before serving. May serve on lettuce leaf cups.

Lowcountry Figs
Yields 6 to 8 servings

1 to 2 pounds fresh figs, large if possible
¼ cup powdered sugar
2 tablespoons rum
1 cup Crème Fraîche (see page 19)
Mint leaves for garnish

Cut figs in half lengthwise. Place cut side up in a 9-by-13-inch dish. Sprinkle with sugar and rum. Cover and refrigerate for several hours. At serving time, place figs and the liquid in dessert bowls or long-stemmed glasses. Top with Crème Fraîche. Garnish with mint leaf and serve.

Brandy Snaps
Yields 18 3½-inch cookies

½ cup (1 stick) butter
¼ cup granulated sugar
¼ cup brown sugar
⅓ cup dark molasses
¼ teaspoon ginger
½ teaspoon cinnamon
¼ teaspoon lemon rind
1 cup flour
2 teaspoons brandy

In a large saucepan over low heat, mix together the butter, sugars, molasses and spices. Remove from heat and add flour and brandy. Roll into 1¼-inch balls. Bake on ungreased cookie sheet at 300° for 12 minutes. Carefully remove from pan. Store in a tightly covered tin.

FACING PAGE

Pleasure boats ply in the harbor once filled with trading vessels. Boiled Peanuts, Roast Beef Pockets and Shrimp Boats make a delightful supper on this summer sunset cruise.

Amid cherished heirloom furniture and pictures, tea sandwiches and confections worthy of a loyalist are laid on a Hepplewhite table in the drawing room of the Philip Porcher house.

Afternoon Tea
The Philip Porcher House

THE DRINKING OF TEA became fashionable in smart English circles in the 1670's and 1680's. Few social customs have had such a profound effect on the development of furniture and silver forms and the way in which rooms were used. By the mid-eighteenth century, it was customary for English ladies to retire for tea in the drawing room following dinner. In 1752, when building his splendid Worcestershire country seat, Hagley Hall, Lord Lyttelton wrote his architect that "Lady Lyttelton wishes for a room of separation between the eating room and the drawing room, to hinder the ladies from the noise and talk of the men when left to their bottle, which must sometimes happen, even at Hagley." Four years later, Lord Lyttelton's epicurean younger brother, William Henry Lyttelton, arrived in Charleston as South Carolina's third royal governor. Like imported royal governors, imported English customs were emulated by fashion-conscious Charlestonians.

As in England, the early Charleston dining room was thought of as a mainly masculine room while the drawing room was considered mainly feminine. Inventories for Charleston's drawing rooms list tea china and silver tea and coffee urns in abundance. Here, the ladies withdrew for polite conversation following the dessert course, or met in the afternoon as teas became separate rituals disassociated with other meals. So established was the ladies' tea in Charleston by 1796 that Josephine duPont complained in a

The border above is from a design in the Philip Porcher house.

letter to a French friend, "This place offers no resources for making close friends. One must be resigned to preparing endless as well as ruinously expensive toilettes in order to partake of their sumptuous teas or else stay absolutely alone."

When, in 1774, the men of Charleston joined in, it was for a tea party of quite a different nature. Fearing an act similar to that of the Boston rebels the previous year, Charleston merchants for whom a shipment of tea was intended were forced to dump it in the river as an "oblation to Neptune."

Philip Porcher, who built this house about 1765, remained a loyalist during the American Revolution. However, his property was not confiscated as was the property of many loyalists following the war. Built on a plan similar to many colonial Carolina plantation houses, the handsome frame dwelling sits on a high basement in which servants' rooms were originally located.

Inside, the Porcher house retains its splendid Georgian raised paneling of cypress, updated in the early nineteenth century by the addition of a neoclassical mantel and a magnificent decorative fanlight opening leading into the stair hall. Recent restoration revealed the tiled fireplace jamb decoration of imported Dutch delftware tiles. The floor plan is somewhat unusual in that both reception rooms are on the first floor rather than the second, the more usual Charleston custom.

AFTERNOON TEA

Serves 25

Russian Tea
Asparagus Canapés
Aunt Lee's Chicken Salad Tarts
Cheese Straws
Vegetable Canapés
Shrimp Paste Finger Sandwiches
Meringued Nuts
Date Nut Bread with Ginger Spread
World's Best Benne Wafers
Heavenly Bars
Bourbon Balls

Russian Tea

Yields 35 to 40 6-ounce servings

4 quarts water
3 cups sugar
1 large tea bag or three small tea bags
Juice of 3 lemons
1 46-ounce can pineapple juice
1 46-ounce can orange juice
1 tablespoon whole cloves

Bring one quart of water to a boil with sugar and tea bag. Remove from heat and allow to steep for 5 minutes. Remove tea bag; return to heat. Add remaining water and fruit juices. Place cloves in a cloth bag or teaball. Add to tea about 15 minutes before serving. Remove cloves before serving.

Asparagus Canapés

Yields 4 dozen

12 to 14 slices thin white bread
3 to 4 tablespoons mayonnaise
¾ teaspoon horseradish
¾ teaspoon Dijon mustard
1 16-ounce can asparagus tips, drained
12 to 13 slices bacon, cut into fourths

Cut bread into small rounds, about 4 per slice; toast. Mix mayonnaise with horseradish and mustard; spread on toasted bread. Partially cook bacon; cut asparagus tips into 1½-inch lengths. Place one piece of asparagus on each round; cover with one piece of bacon and broil until crisp—about 3 minutes. Serve immediately.

Aunt Lee's
Chicken Salad Tarts

Yields 24 tarts

2 cups cooked cubed chicken
1 cup diced celery
¾ to 1 cup mayonnaise
2 tablespoons lemon juice
½ to 1 teaspoon salt
¼ teaspoon white pepper
¼ cup chopped pickles, optional
24 Tart Shells

Mix ingredients together and chill until ready to serve. Spoon into Tart Shells.

TART SHELLS
  Yields 24 1½-inch tart shells

1½ cups flour
Pinch of salt
6 tablespoons (¾ stick) butter
2 tablespoons vegetable shortening
3 tablespoons cold water

In bowl of food processor, using steel blade, combine flour, salt, butter and vegetable shortening. Pulse for several seconds until crumbly. Add water and blend until dough forms a ball. Wrap in plastic wrap and refrigerate overnight. Dough can be kept in refrigerator for several days. To roll, bring dough to a workable temperature. For 1½-inch tarts, divide dough into 24 portions; for 3½-inch tarts, divide dough into 6 portions. On a floured surface, roll each portion of dough into a circle. Place in a tart pan, trim excess. Bake 350° for 10 to 15 min-

utes or until pale and crisp. Cool completely in pans; may refrigerate.

Cheese Straws
Yields 5 to 6 dozen

1 pound extra-sharp Cheddar cheese
1 pound (4 sticks) butter
1 teaspoon salt
½ teaspoon red pepper
¼ teaspoon paprika
4 cups plain flour

Cream cheese and butter. Add salt, pepper and paprika. Gradually add flour until all is incorporated. Put in cookie press and press onto ungreased cookie sheet. Bake at 375° for 10 to 15 minutes. Cheese straws can be frozen or kept in a tin.

Vegetable Canapés
Yields 4 to 5 dozen canapés

8 ounces cream cheese, softened
1 teaspoon lemon juice
1 medium onion, grated
¾ cup finely chopped or ground carrots
  or green pepper
1 tablespoon mayonnaise
1 teaspoon celery seed
2 small cucumbers, sliced
2 small squash, sliced
2 small zucchini, sliced

Combine first six ingredients and mix well; chill. To serve, spread on top of veg-

etable slices or place mixture in pastry tube with desired tip and pipe mixture onto vegetable slices—cucumber, squash, snow peas or other vegetables.

Shrimp Paste Finger Sandwiches
Yields 16 to 18 small sandwiches

8 ounces cream cheese
1 tablespoon lemon juice
1 tablespoon mayonnaise
¼ teaspoon onion powder
Dash of hot sauce
Pinch of mace
Dash of garlic salt
1 cup finely chopped cooked shrimp
  (½ pound)

Soften cream cheese; add lemon juice and mayonnaise and blend in seasonings. Add shrimp. This mixture can be molded or rolled into small balls, covered with either chopped parsley or toasted benne seed, or used as a filling for sandwiches.

Meringued Nuts
Yields 2 cups

1 egg white
½ cup packed light brown sugar
Dash of salt
2 cups pecan halves

In a small bowl, beat egg white until stiff. Add brown sugar and salt. Gently stir in

pecan halves, coating each pecan half thoroughly with egg-white mixture. Remove each coated nut to a foil-lined, ungreased cookie sheet. Bake at 250° for 30 minutes. Turn oven off and leave for 30 minutes. Remove nuts from oven; cool. Store in airtight container.

Date Nut Bread

Yields 1 loaf

3 tablespoons butter, softened
1 cup chopped dates
¼ cup brown sugar
⅓ cup sugar
¾ cup boiling water
1 egg
¼ cup milk
2 cups flour
2 teaspoons baking powder
½ teaspoon salt
¾ cup chopped nuts
1 teaspoon vanilla extract
2 tablespoons brandy
Ginger Spread

Place the butter, dates and sugars in a large mixing bowl; add boiling water and let the mixture stand for 15 minutes. Stir. Add egg and milk. Sift flour, baking powder and salt together; add to mixture. Stir in nuts, vanilla and brandy. Pour mixture into a greased 9-by-5-inch loaf pan. Bake at 350° for 40 minutes. Bread is easier to slice if refrigerated overnight. Serve with Ginger Spread.

Ginger Spread

Yields 1½ cups

8 ounces cream cheese, softened
4 ounces ginger marmalade
½ cup chopped nuts
Mayonnaise, enough to mix well

Combine ingredients; mix well and spread on thinly sliced Date Nut Bread. Spread is also good with Banana, Cranberry or Orange Bread.

World's Best Benne Wafers

Yields 3 dozen

½ cup (1 stick) butter
½ cup dark corn syrup
¼ cup firmly packed brown sugar
¾ cup all purpose flour
½ cup toasted benne seeds or sesame seeds

Preheat oven to 375°. Cover a baking sheet with foil and grease generously. Combine butter, syrup and brown sugar in a small saucepan. Place over medium heat and stir until butter melts. Mix in flour. Bring to a boil, stirring constantly. Remove from heat and stir in benne seeds. Let stand until slightly thickened but still warm. Mixture must not cool. Place saucepan in another pan of water and keep over low heat to maintain proper consistency. Drop batter by scant half-teaspoonfuls onto baking sheet, leaving a

lot of space for wafer to expand. Bake for 4 to 5 minutes until bubbly and golden. Watch closely to prevent burning. Let cool for 1 to 2 minutes until set; remove foil to a wire rack to finish cooling. Carefully peel away foil. Store in airtight container.

Note: Do not substitute margarine for butter.

Heavenly Bars

Yields 2 to 3 dozen

⅓ cup butter
1½ cups firmly packed brown sugar,
    divided
1 cup plus 2 tablespoons flour
2 eggs
1 teaspoon vanilla extract
½ teaspoon salt
1 teaspoon baking powder
1⅓ cups shredded coconut
¾ to 1 cup chopped pecans
Orange Butter Frosting

In food processor, using steel blade, blend together the butter, ½ cup sugar and 1 cup flour until mixture resembles fine crumbs. Press mixture over the bottom of a greased 9-by-13-inch pan. Bake at 350° for 10 minutes. Let cool for 10 minutes. In a mixing bowl, beat eggs until thick and lemon colored. Gradually add remaining sugar and flour. Add vanilla, salt, baking soda, coconut and nuts. Pour coconut mixture over baked crust. Return to oven and bake for 20 minutes or until

top is golden brown. When cooled, frost with Orange Butter Frosting. Cut into bars.

Orange Butter Frosting

¼ cup (½ stick) butter, softened
2 cups powdered sugar
1 teaspoon vanilla
¾ teaspoon orange peel
1 to 2 tablespoons orange juice

In small bowl, beat together butter and powdered sugar. Add the vanilla and orange peel. Add enough orange juice to make a good spreading consistency. Spread over cooled Heavenly Bars.

Bourbon Balls

Yields 6 dozen 1½-inch balls

1 cup (2 sticks) butter, softened
2 pounds 10–X confectioners' sugar
½ cup good bourbon
2 cups finely chopped pecans

Mix together butter and confectioners' sugar. Gradually add bourbon and chopped pecans. Mix until thoroughly blended. Refrigerate for several hours. Remove from refrigerator; form into balls 1 to 1½ inches in diameter. Place on cookie sheets; return to freezer until ready to dip into Chocolate Glaze.

Note: Do not substitute margarine for butter.

Chocolate Glaze

⅓ bar paraffin or 3 tablespoons vegetable
  shortening
2 12-ounce packages chocolate chips

In heavy saucepan, over medium heat, melt together paraffin and chocolate chips. Stir until completely blended and chocolate is melted. Dip each Bourbon Ball into mixture and return to cookie sheet. Refrigerate until ready to serve.

Note: Chocolate mixture must be kept warm in order for balls to be dipped.

Game Supper
The Heyward-Washington House

WHEN PRESIDENT George Washington visited Charleston in May 1791, he used as his official residence the house now known as the Heyward-Washington House. Built between 1772 and 1773 by Daniel Heyward for his son Thomas, one of South Carolina's four signers of the Declaration of Independence, it is a fine example of the Charleston "double" house. In 1792, when Thomas Heyward advertised the property for sale, it was described as having "twelve rooms with a fireplace in each, a cellar and loft; a kitchen for cooking and washing, with a cellar below and five rooms for servants above; a carriage house and stables, all of brick surrounded by brick walls." Now a property of the Charleston Museum, the house and its dependencies present a good picture of early Charleston's town house complexes.

The rigors of colonial cookery are suggested by the kitchen building, which probably predates the main house. In the course of the archaeological dig on the site, over 88,000 artifacts were uncovered. This investigation also found that two previous houses had existed on the property, one of frame construction and one of brick. The surviving kitchen and laundry building more than likely belonged to the second of these, built by John Milner, a gunsmith and blacksmith.

While supervised by the mistress of the house, the kitchens of well-to-do Charlestonians were the domain of servants, nearly always black female slaves. There can be no doubt that this group comprised the largest contingent of skilled chefs in the Lowcoun-

try, and early documents confirm that specialization did exist. For example, the 1821 inventory of the estate of Mrs. Lucretia C. Radcliffe included among her thirty-seven slaves "Judy (a cook), Scipio (a cook), Rachael (a pastry cook — infirm) and James (head waiter)."

Popular early dishes included those produced from game, pursued for sport by generations of imported South Carolinians, and for centuries before that by the native Indian population. Before the advent of the whites, Native Americans had used bows and arrows for hunting, but quickly came to prefer guns. The white-tailed deer was a staple, providing both food and clothing for Carolina Indians. Herds of deer were artificially increased through the burning of woods, which kept down the underbrush and promoted the growth of grass.

With the settlement of Charleston and its emergence as a trading port city, deerskins became one of the most important commodities. It is estimated that several million deer were killed to supply the insatiable desire for buckskin breeches among the British. In 1748 alone, Indians supplied 160,000 skins for export from Charleston, often leaving the carcasses to rot.

Carolina birds were prized for both their edible and their decorative qualities. Geese, turkeys, quail and ducks were favored on dinner tables, but nonpareils, cardinals and bluebirds often ended up in decorative cages. In 1750, Peter Manigault wrote from London to his mother in Carolina, "Mrs. Brailsford . . . brought the Red birds you were so kind to send me as far as Dover, but in coming to London, the Poor creatures died in the Post Chaise." American birds were obviously novelties in Europe, and in Charleston there are many early references to birds as pets. One of the most interesting is Josiah Quincy's account of a bird at dinner in Miles Brewton's splendid dining room on King Street: "A very fine bird kept familiarly playing over the room, under our chairs and the table, picking up the crumbs, etc., and perching on the window, side board and chairs: vastly pretty!"

GAME SUPPER

Serves 6 to 8

Hot Buttered Rum
Edmund's Quail Appetizers
Pheasant Cheese Ball
Roast Goose with Apple Chestnut Stuffing
Duck Flambé
Last Resort Plantation's Doves
Mrs. G's Red Rice
Suzanne's Cauliflower with Spinach Sauce
Harvest Salad with Tangy French Dressing
Herbed Loaves
Apple Torte

Hot Buttered Rum Mix
Yields 1½ quarts

1 pound (4 sticks) butter
1½ teaspoons cinnamon
½ teaspoon ground cloves
½ teaspoon ground nutmeg
1 teaspoon allspice
2 pounds brown sugar
3 eggs, beaten

Melt butter in saucepan and add spices. Pour over sugar in large mixing bowl. Add eggs and beat with electric mixer until well blended and very thick. This mix may be kept in the freezer for months. To make Hot Buttered Rum, place 1 heaping tablespoon of mix in mug with 1 ounce rum and fill with boiling water.

Edmund's Quail Appetizers
Yields 12 servings

3 quail, cleaned and split into halves
16 ounces Italian salad dressing

Marinate quail in salad dressing overnight. On charcoal or gas grill, cook 5 to 7 minutes on first side. Turn and cook another 4 to 6 minutes. When done, split the halves and serve; just pick up with fingers and nibble meat from the bone. These may be served with Spicy Mustard; see page 16. Be sure to provide a waste bowl for bones.

Pheasant Cheese Ball
Yields 20 to 25 servings

1 5-ounce jar Old English Spread
¼ pound very sharp Cheddar cheese, grated
4 ounces blue cheese, crumbled
4 ounces cream cheese, softened
¼ cup mayonnaise
2 teaspoons Worcestershire sauce
1 tablespoon finely chopped onion
1 tablespoon finely chopped sweet pickle
¼ cup finely chopped parsley
⅛ teaspoon cayenne pepper
⅔ to 1 cup sliced almonds, optional
⅓ cup slivered almonds

In a large bowl, mix together the cheeses, cream cheese, mayonnaise, Worcestershire sauce, onion, pickle, parsley and pepper. Form into a pheasant shape with a body and head—a large oval ball and a small round ball. Cover the body with sliced almonds, carefully placed; use slivered almonds for the wings. For the tail, thread black or green olives on various-length wooden skewers. Place greenery such as fresh parsley around the body. Serve with crackers.

Roast Goose with Apple Chestnut Stuffing
Yields 6 to 8 servings

1 12- to 14-pound goose
White wine
Apple Chestnut Stuffing

Wipe goose clean; reserve liver. Rub goose inside and out with salt. Stuff bird with Apple Chestnut Stuffing. Prick goose with a fork a few times; place on a rack in a roasting pan. Cook at 400° for 20 minutes; reduce to 325° and continue cooking for 20 minutes per pound. Baste goose with white wine and skim off fat intermittently.

APPLE CHESTNUT STUFFING
  Yields 8 cups

2½ pounds chestnuts
½ cup chopped onion
½ cup (1 stick) butter
4 cups peeled, chopped apples
1 cup parboiled, seedless raisins,
  drained and dried
Liver from a 12- to 14-pound goose,
  chopped
2 cooked potatoes, diced
1½ teaspoons salt
¼ teaspoon pepper
¼ cup chopped parsley
½ teaspoon each of sage, mace, nutmeg
  and cloves

Cover chestnuts with boiling water; simmer for 15 to 25 minutes. Drain; remove shells and skins. Chop and set aside. Sauté onion in butter until transparent. Add apples, chestnuts, raisins, goose liver and potatoes. Sauté until apples are soft and mixture is light brown. Remove stuffing from heat and add salt, pepper, parsley and spices.

Duck Flambé
Yields 6 servings

3 ducks
1 6-ounce can frozen orange juice
  concentrate
2½ cups water
1 cup powdered sugar
½ teaspoon salt
½ teaspoon pepper
½ teaspoon ground ginger
½ teaspoon thyme
1 tablespoon cornstarch
1 orange
1 lemon
1 apple, sliced
1 onion, sliced
⅓ cup cognac

Clean and halve ducks and set aside. Mix together the orange juice, water, sugar, salt, pepper, ginger, thyme and cornstarch; add 1 teaspoon grated rind and juice squeezed from lemon and orange. Cook over medium heat, stirring constantly until mixture thickens and boils; remove from heat. Slice the remainder of the orange and lemon. Place birds skin side down and stuff cavity with slices of apple, onion, orange and lemon. Fill cavity with sauce. Cover tightly or wrap birds individually in foil. Bake for 30 minutes at 425°. Remove birds from sauce and broil them on a cookie sheet, skin side up, until skin is brown and crisp. Keep the sauce and fruit warm. To serve, put the birds on a large platter, cover with sauce, add cognac and flame.
Note: Allow one-half duck per person.

Last Resort Plantation's Doves
Yields 6 servings

12 doves, dressed
Salt and pepper to taste
¼ to ½ cup flour
1 cup (2 sticks) butter
2 cups chicken broth

Salt, pepper and lightly flour doves. Sauté in butter to brown on all sides. With breast side down, cover with chicken broth and simmer covered for 1 hour until birds are tender. Add water if needed, and turn birds to prevent sticking.

Mrs. G's Red Rice
Yields 6 to 8 servings

6 slices bacon, cut into small pieces
1 onion, chopped
2 stalks celery, chopped
1 small green pepper, chopped
1 16-ounce can tomatoes
½ teaspoon salt
½ teaspoon pepper
½ teaspoon Worcestershire sauce
¼ teaspoon Tabasco sauce
½ teaspoon sugar
2 cups raw rice

Begin frying bacon. When bacon is partially cooked, pour off bacon drippings, leaving enough to sauté onions, celery and green pepper. Add onions to the bacon; sauté. When onions are almost transparent, add celery and green pepper and sauté. Place a colander over frying pan; pour tomatoes into colander and mash. Empty contents of colander into the bacon mixture. Season with salt, pepper, Worcestershire, Tabasco and sugar. Simmer for 10 minutes.

Wash rice in top of rice steamer. Add tomato mixture and cook for 30 minutes. Remove top of steamer from heat and fluff rice with fork. Add 1 tablespoon cold water. Return to heat and cook 15 to 30 minutes longer. Be sure to check water in bottom of steamer.

Suzanne's Cauliflower with Spinach Sauce
Yields 6 to 8 servings

1 large head cauliflower
1 10-ounce package frozen,
*   chopped spinach*
2 to 3 tablespoons butter
½ cup half-and-half
2 tablespoons flour
1 cup grated Swiss cheese
Freshly grated nutmeg

Wash cauliflower and cut into flowerets. Steam; set aside. In large saucepan, thaw spinach in butter. Add half-and-half, flour, cheese and nutmeg. Stir until thick-

ened. Place cauliflower flowerets in serving dish. Pour spinach mixture over cauliflower. Serve immediately.

Harvest Salad
Yields 6 to 8 servings

1 head lettuce
3 fresh pears, sliced into wedges
1 small purple onion, sliced into rings
2 to 3 ounces Saga blue cheese
Tangy French Dressing

Line salad plate with lettuce; arrange pear slices, onion, and thin slice of Saga blue cheese on lettuce. Top with Tangy French Dressing.

Tangy French Dressing
Yields 3 cups

1 garlic clove, chopped
1 teaspoon salt
1 teaspoon pepper
¾ teaspoon paprika
½ teaspoon dry mustard
1 small onion, chopped
1 10 ¾-ounce can condensed tomato soup
1 cup vegetable oil
½ cup sugar
½ cup vinegar
1 teaspoon Worcestershire sauce
Dash cayenne

Combine all ingredients in a jar and shake well to blend. Do not use blender. Refrigerate.

Herbed Loaves
Yields 6 to 8 servings

4 ounces cream cheese, softened
2 tablespoons butter, softened
1 teaspoon dried parsley flakes
1 teaspoon grated onion
½ teaspoon caraway seeds
⅛ teaspoon garlic powder
1 8-ounce package refrigerated crescent rolls
1 egg yolk, beaten
1 tablespoon water
½ teaspoon poppy seeds

Combine cream cheese, butter, parsley, onion, caraway seeds and garlic powder in a small bowl; set aside. Unroll crescent rolls into two rectangles; connect ends to make one large rectangle, pressing to seal. Spread cream cheese mixture to within ½ inch of edge. Roll jelly-roll fashion, starting at long side; pinch to seal. Place on greased baking sheet. Using scissors, slice dough at ½-inch intervals, being careful not to cut completely through the dough. Pull out alternating sides to expose the jelly-roll pattern. Beat egg yolk with water. Brush top with egg and sprinkle with poppy seeds. Bake at 350° for 20 minutes.

Apple Torte
Yields 8 servings

CRUST

½ cup (1 stick) butter
½ cup sugar
¼ teaspoon vanilla extract
1 cup flour

Cream butter, sugar and vanilla together. Blend in flour and spread dough onto bottom and halfway up sides of a 9-inch springform pan. Bake 5 minutes at 350°.

FILLING

8 ounces cream cheese, softened
¼ cup sugar
1 egg
½ teaspoon vanilla

Combine softened cream cheese, sugar, egg and vanilla. Blend until thoroughly mixed. Pour mixture over crust.

TOPPING

⅓ cup sugar
½ teaspoon cinnamon
4 cups peeled and thinly sliced apples
¼ cup slivered almonds

In a large bowl, combine sugar, cinnamon and apples. Toss gently until thoroughly mixed. Arrange apples on top of cream cheese mixture in design of your choice. Sprinkle almonds on top. Bake at 350° for 25 to 30 minutes or until center is set. Cool before removing sides of pan.

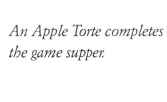

*An Apple Torte completes
the game supper.*

*The efforts involved in colonial cookery are apparent
in the kitchen house of the Heyward-Washington
property on Church Street.*

*Herbed Loaves and
Duck Flambé served on
a pewter platter.*

The Middleton Place Hounds prepare for a hunt on the grounds of one of America's most historic plantations.

Venison Grillades on Hominy, Mixed Greens and Apple Ring Fritters await riders after the hunt.

Hunt Breakfast
Middleton Place

TALLYHO! The call of the huntsman at the sight of a fox. The Middleton Place Hounds have occasionally stalked the fox, but the plantation terrain has also provided more exotic prey, including a bobcat and even an alligator. Most hunts at Middleton Place are drag hunts, the artificial scent of the fox being dragged in a burlap bag across a devised route.

Organized in 1973, the Middleton Place Hounds carry on a centuries-old British and Southern tradition. The season begins on the first Sunday after Thanksgiving and lasts through mid-March with the hounds going out three times each week. During formal hunts, the scene is spectacular, with members wearing black coats with buff britches or white britches and scarlet coats, the famous "pink" coat named for the London tailor who first designed them. The reward at the end of the hunt is a generous hunt breakfast served in front of the historic Middleton Place house.

Such English country pursuits seem entirely at home at Middleton. The Duke de la Rochefoucauld-Liancourt visited Middleton Place in 1798 and recorded, "The ensemble of these buildings calls to recollection the ancient English country seats." The main house at Middleton Place had been built sometime before 1741 by either John Williams or his son-in-law Henry Middleton. A speaker of the Commons, Commissioner for Indian Affairs, a member of the Governor's Council and, later, second president of the First Continental Congress, Henry Middleton owned some twenty planta-

tions, 50,000 acres of land and 800 slaves. Later Middletons carried on the legacy of political involvement and diplomatic service. Henry's son Arthur was a signer of the Declaration of Independence; his grandson, also named Henry, was a governor of South Carolina and America's first minister to Russia. Henry's great-grandson, Williams, signed the Ordinance of Secession and suffered the indignity of finding his venerable plantation house burned beyond repair in 1865, the victim of General Sherman's troops. Williams Middleton rebuilt the south flanker after the Civil War and today it is open to the public, a repository for surviving family furniture, paintings, silver, and books interpreting the history of this remarkable American family.

The magnificent gardens of the plantation are the great glory of Middleton Place. Laid out in the formal axial plan favored in early eighteenth-century Europe, they represent one of the earliest and certainly one of the most ambitious schemes of early landscape gardening in America. Unlike many of its neighbors, Middleton Place enjoyed a commanding position on high land a quarter of a mile from the Ashley River. Henry Middleton took full advantage of its site, creating a series of sweeping terraces which descend to artificial decorative lakes and the river and marshland beyond. It is this juxtaposition of the natural and formal, nature and the imitation of nature, which gives the garden its great spatial and visual complexity.

Through the years, successive owners have added new varieties of plants, including the camellia japonica which French botanist André Michaux planted in the garden in 1786, its first use in any American garden. Azaleas were added in the mid-nineteenth century and again in the early 1930's when 35,000 azaleas of many varieties were planted on the wooded hillside above the old rice mill. In earlier times, the garden contained a number of important statues strategically placed in focal points of the garden. German sculptor Johann Gottfried Schadow's graceful marble *Wood Nymph* is the sole survivor, the others having been destroyed or otherwise lost.

Middleton Place is by no means a static museum. Wildlife and fowl abound, the plantation stable yard is busy the year round, and events such as the meets of the Middleton Place Hounds infuse life into this still quite active Lowcountry plantation.

HUNT BREAKFAST

Serves 16

Bocci Ball Punch
Eggplant Caviar
Venison Grillades
Hominy
Apple Ring Fritters
Mixed Greens
French Bread *
Dot's Pecan Pie • Brown Sugar Pie
Brandied Coffee

* See page 110.

Bocci Ball Punch

Yields 20 6-ounce servings

Ice ring
2 quarts orange juice, chilled
1 6-ounce can frozen orange juice
  concentrate
1 pint vodka
1½ cups Amaretto
1 quart sparkling water, chilled

To make ice ring: Partially freeze ½-inch layer of water in a 1- to 1½-quart ring mold. Remove from freezer and arrange fruits and leaves in a wreath design. Return to freezer to allow to set. Cover with ice-cold water to fill mold. Return to freezer for several days before using. Dip in warm water to unmold.

Mix together orange juice, orange juice concentrate, vodka and Amaretto. Add to punch bowl. Just before serving add ice ring and sparkling water. Serve in mint julep cups.

Eggplant Caviar

Yields 2 to 3 cups

1 large eggplant, about 2 pounds
1 cup finely chopped onion
6 tablespoons olive oil, divided
½ cup finely chopped green pepper
1 teaspoon finely chopped garlic
2 large ripe tomatoes, peeled, seeded
  and chopped
½ teaspoon sugar
2 teaspoons salt

Freshly ground pepper
2 to 3 tablespoons lemon juice

Preheat oven to 425°. Bake the eggplant on a rack in the center of the oven for one hour, turning it once or twice, until it is soft and the skin is charred. Meanwhile, in a large saucepan, cook the onions in 4 tablespoons olive oil until they are soft, but not brown. Stir in the green pepper and garlic and cook for another 5 minutes; scrape the pan. Remove the skin from the eggplant and chop the pulp to almost a puree. Add the eggplant to the onion mixture. Stir in the tomatoes, sugar, salt and pepper. Heat the remaining 2 tablespoons olive oil and pour in the eggplant mixture. Bring to a boil, stirring constantly; turn heat to low and cover. Cook until all moisture has evaporated and the mixture is thick enough to hold its shape in a spoon. Stir in 2 tablespoons lemon juice and taste for seasoning. Chill the mixture and serve with dark rye, pumpernickel or sesame crackers.

Venison Grillades

Yields 16 servings

4 pounds venison stew meat
¼ to ⅓ cup bacon drippings
⅓ cup flour
1 quart water
2½ cups red wine
¾ cup chopped onion
2½ to 3 cups green pepper strips
3 cloves garlic, minced
1 pound carrots, peeled and sliced

3 bay leaves
1 tablespoon thyme
⅓ cup chopped parsley
1 teaspoon freshly ground black pepper
2 teaspoons salt
¼ teaspoon cayenne
¼ cup tomato paste
2 4-ounce jars pearl onions
Hominy

Cut venison into 1-inch cubes. Brown meat in bacon drippings; remove meat from pan. Stir flour into hot pan drippings to make a dark-brown roux. Add water and red wine, chopped onion, pepper strips, garlic, carrots, bay leaves, thyme, parsley, pepper, salt, cayenne, and tomato paste. Cook 3 to 5 minutes, then add meat. Simmer covered for 1 to 2 hours. Add pearl onions and heat thoroughly. Grillades should be very tender. Serve over Hominy or rice.

Hominy
Yields 16 servings

2½ quarts water
1 tablespoon salt
2½ cups quick grits
2 cups milk
¾ cup (1½ sticks) butter

Bring water to a boil; add salt. Stir grits slowly into water. Return to a boil; reduce heat and cover. Simmer for 5 minutes, stirring occasionally. Stir in butter and milk; simmer for 5 minutes or until thickened.

Apple Ring Fritters
Yields 16 to 20 fritters

1 cup flour
1½ teaspoons baking powder
2 tablespoons sugar
½ teaspoon salt
¾ cup milk
1 egg
4 large apples
Vegetable shortening
¼ cup sugar
1 teaspoon cinnamon

Sift dry ingredients together. Add milk and egg. Beat well and set aside. Peel, core and slice apples into rings ¼ inch thick. Add enough shortening in frying pan to achieve a depth of 1½ inches. Dip rings in batter and drop into hot shortening. Fry until golden brown. Drain on paper towel. Mix sugar and cinnamon together and sprinkle over fritters.

Mixed Greens
Yields 16 servings

1 small cured ham hock
2 quarts water
1 to 1½ pounds kale
1 to 1½ pounds turnip greens
1 to 1½ pounds of any other greens, except
*   collards or spinach*

Wash ham hock and place in 2 quarts of water in a large stock pot. Bring to a boil. Reduce heat and simmer for 30 to 40 minutes or until ham hock is tender. Add

more water if necessary. Wash and trim greens. Add greens to stock pot; cook until tender, 1 to 2 hours. When done, discard ham hock; serve or refrigerate and reheat. Greens will freeze well. Mustard greens, land cress and Swiss chard are especially good.

Dot's Pecan Pie

Yields 1 9-inch pie

3 eggs
¾ cup dark corn syrup
½ cup (1 stick) margarine, melted
½ cup sugar
1 tablespoon self-rising flour
1 teaspoon vanilla
¼ teaspoon salt
1 cup chopped pecans
1 9-inch deep-dish pie shell

Preheat oven to 450°. Mix all ingredients well and pour into unbaked 9-inch deep-dish pie shell. Bake at 450° for 10 minutes, then turn oven down to 350° and continue baking for another 20 to 25 minutes.

Brown Sugar Pie

Yields 2 9-inch pies

1 pound light brown sugar
½ cup (1 stick) margarine or butter,
  softened
3 eggs
1 teaspoon vanilla
2 9-inch pie shells

Cream sugar and butter until fluffy. Add eggs and beat lightly; add vanilla. Pour into two unbaked 9-inch pie shells. Bake at 350° for 45 minutes or until center is firm. Watch crust carefully; covering edge with foil will prevent overbrowning. Freezes well.

Brandied Coffee

Yields 1 serving

1 cup coffee
1 ounce brandy
1 to 2 tablespoons sugar

Stir brandy and sugar into coffee and serve.

Thanksgiving Dinner
The Nathaniel Russell House

THANKSGIVING has been celebrated in one form or another since 1621, when Governor William Bradford of the Plymouth Colony issued a Thanksgiving proclamation following the survival of the colony's first bitter winter. It was not a generally recognized holiday throughout the colonial period and was celebrated only sporadically and in various months including January, October and December. On November 26, 1789, President George Washington called for a nationwide day of Thanksgiving, making it clear that the day should be one of prayer and giving thanks to God. Abraham Lincoln would later declare the last Thursday in November Thanksgiving Day, and Franklin D. Roosevelt adjusted this to the fourth rather than the last Thursday — an encouragement to holiday shopping in Depression-ridden America. One constant throughout these various observances has been the eating of turkey as the main course, which took on special meaning during the Revolutionary period as a repudiation of beef, the British staple.

Nathaniel Russell's ancestry was deeply rooted in the New England of the pilgrims, his great-great-grandfather, John Russell, having been made a freeman of Cambridge, Massachusetts, in 1636. Nathaniel Russell would later become a founder and first president of Charleston's New England Society, a fraternal and philanthropic organization of Charlestonians with New England ancestry that still thrives today.

A native of Bristol, Rhode Island, Russell arrived in Charleston as a young man in 1765 as an agent for northern merchants and advertised in the *South Carolina Gazette*:

> Nathaniel Russell has just imported, in the sloop Defiance, from
> Rhode Island, a parcel of good Horses, Northward Rum, cheese,
> sperma-coated candles, onions and a few barrels of Apples, which he
> will sell cheap at his store in Colonel Beale's wharf.

Having established himself as one of Charleston's leading merchants, Nathaniel Russell was probably safeguarding mercantile interests when he spent a Tory's exile in England during the American War of Independence. He returned and repatriated in 1783 and quickly set about amassing a huge fortune in his adopted city.

His marriage in 1788 to Sarah Hopton, daughter of local merchant William Hopton, no doubt aided Russell in re-establishing himself both socially and economically. The couple and their two daughters moved into their newly completed mansion house in the spring of 1808.

Today, the Russell house is owned by the Historic Charleston Foundation and is open daily for guided tours. The spacious interiors are noted for their extraordinary refinement and beautiful Federal-period detail. A magnificent free-flying staircase of elliptical shape affords a processional route to the drawing rooms on the second floor.

The dining room, extended early this century, is on the ground floor and is filled with an important collection of decorative arts, many of Charleston manufacture. A handsome early-nineteenth-century dining table was made for a local plantation as was the early neoclassical sideboard with highly figured, matched mahogany veneers. The English tall-case clock, circa 1760, was imported by local watchmaker Joshua Lockwood who retailed it to an eighteenth-century Charlestonian. Filled with fruit and symbolizing plenty, a 1759 London silver epergne in the rococo style makes a sumptuous centerpiece for this bounteous Thanksgiving feast.

MOST kinds of provisions are much rais'd of late in Charles Town, beef, which on account of the hot weather is now reckoned out of season and but very indifferent can't be had under 4d per pound but in the winter it is much better at 2d per pound. Veal which is sold by the joint comes to about 5d per poind. The town in general is very ill-supplied with fish, wich is not owing to a real scarcity for there are plenty to be caught if there were but proper people to seek after them, but as that is not the case they are scarce and dear: however that is pretty well made up for by having plenty of fine turtle one half the year from 4d to 8d per pound. Poultry is in general very good and reasonable, fine capons being at a shilling a piece and very good fowls fit for the spit at 9d and in the winter season here are fine wild ducks at 4d each, plenty of excellent otter-lines, partridges and quails at 2d each, with abundance of very fine wild turkeys weighing from 20 to 40 pounds from 3 to 5 shillings each, also plenty of venison at a guinea a buck, which tho' it has little or no fat is generally esteem'd very good flafor'd. . . .

"Charleston, S.C., in 1774 as Described by an English Traveller"

THANKSGIVING DINNER

Serves 12

Hot Mulled Cider
Acorn Squash Soup
Roast Turkey • Giblet Gravy
Corn Bread and Sausage Dressing
Oyster Dressing • Saffron Rice
Aunt Lee's Corn Pudding
Turnip Cups with Peas
Brussels Sprouts • Dill Carrots
Cranberry Salad • Rockville Pears
Miss Lucy's Yeast Rolls
Pumpkin Squares • Lane Cake

Hot Mulled Cider

Yields 12 to 14 cups

4½ cups apple cider
⅓ cup sugar
3 sticks cinnamon
12 whole cloves
1½ fifths dry white wine
½ cup lemon juice

In 2-quart saucepan, combine cider, sugar, cinnamon sticks and cloves. Bring to boil, reduce heat and simmer uncovered for 15 to 20 minutes. Remove spices; add wine and lemon juice. Heat thoroughly but do not boil. Serve in punch cups or mugs, garnished with lemon slices or a cinnamon stick.

Acorn Squash Soup

Yields 10 cups

2 acorn squash, about 2 pounds
4 medium onions, coarsely chopped
7 cups chicken broth
⅓ cup chopped parsley
1 cup half-and-half
¼ teaspoon powdered thyme
Salt and pepper to taste

Quarter the squash, remove seeds and membranes. Blanch until rind can easily be separated from pulp. Cube pulp and place in 6-quart saucepan; add onions, chicken broth, salt and pepper. Simmer for 30 minutes. Pour into blender container; add parsley and blend until smooth. (Blend in as many batches as necessary.) Return to saucepan and slowly add half-and-half. Stir in thyme. Correct seasoning.

Roast Turkey

Yields 10 to 12 servings

1 10- to 12-pound fresh turkey
½+ teaspoon salt
½+ teaspoon pepper
½+ teaspoon paprika
¾ cup (1½ sticks) butter

Wash turkey. Sprinkle with salt, pepper and paprika; pat with ¼ cup butter. After turkey has been stuffed, place bird in roasting pan, breast side down. Roast turkey in 325° oven according to the following timetable:

Turkey Roasting Timetable

Weight	Approximate Time	Serves
10 to 12 pounds	4 to 4½ hours	10 to 12
14 to 16 pounds	4½ to 5½ hours	14 to 16
18 to 20 pounds	5½ to 6½ hours	18 to 20

Continued . . .

Melt remaining butter. Add ½ teaspoon salt, ½ teaspoon pepper and ½ teaspoon paprika to butter. Baste turkey with butter mixture every 45 minutes until last hour. During the last hour, take top off of roasting pan and brown for 20 minutes. Baste and turn the bird over; baste the breast side and brown for the last 40 minutes of baking time, basting every 20 minutes.

Giblet Gravy
Yields 1½ pints

Giblets from a 10- to 12-pound turkey
2 stalks celery, chopped
1 medium onion, chopped
1 small bell pepper, chopped
¼ cup flour
Salt and pepper to taste

Simmer giblets in 2 quarts water with celery, onion, bell pepper and seasoning for approximately 2 hours, adding additional water if necessary. Mix flour with ½ cup water until flour has dissolved; pour through a strainer. Add to giblet mixture. This may be repeated if thicker gravy is desired. Add pan drippings from roasted turkey for a heartier flavor.

Corn Bread and Sausage Dressing
Yields 5 cups

1 pound bulk sausage
½ cup chopped parsley

5 medium onions, chopped
3 cups chopped celery
½ cup (1 stick) butter
6 eggs, beaten
1 cup half-and-half
¼ cup chicken stock
1 teaspoon poultry seasoning
5 cups corn bread crumbs (see page 9)

Cook sausage and drain well. Sauté parsley, onions and celery in butter until tender. Combine sausage and parsley mixture with the remaining ingredients and stuff inside both cavities of a 10- to 20-pound turkey. Any leftovers may be baked in greased dish at 325°. Baking time depends on the amount; do not overcook.

Oyster Dressing
Yields 5 cups

1 pint standard oysters
¾ cup chopped celery
½ cup chopped onion
4 to 5 tablespoons butter
6 cups white bread cubes
½ teaspoon salt
½ teaspoon freshly ground pepper
½ teaspoon poultry seasoning

Drain oysters, reserving ¼ cup liquid; coarsely chop oysters and set aside. Sauté celery and onions in butter until tender. Add this mixture to bread cubes, oysters and oyster liquid. Add remaining ingredients. Toss to mix well. Spoon dressing into greased 9-by-13-inch baking dish.

Bake at 325° for 30 to 45 minutes or until set. (This should be served immediately; it does not keep well.)

Saffron Rice

Yields 12 servings

3¼ cups chicken stock
¾ cup dry white wine
½ to 1 teaspoon powdered saffron
Salt and pepper to taste
2 cups white rice

Bring chicken stock to a boil in a large saucepan. Dissolve saffron in wine and stir into stock. Season with salt and pepper and add rice. Cover pan and simmer until all the liquid is absorbed and rice is tender, about 30 minutes.

Aunt Lee's Corn Pudding

Yields 12 servings

4 cups fresh, sweet corn, cut off cob,
*   or frozen corn kernels*
4 eggs, beaten
1½ cups milk
½ teaspoon salt
¼ teaspoon white pepper
1 teaspoon sugar, optional
¼ cup (½ stick) butter

In a large bowl, mix together the corn, eggs, milk, salt, pepper and sugar. Pour

into a buttered 2-quart flat casserole dish. Dot the top with butter. Bake at 325° for 1 hour. Stir the corn one or two times during the baking process.

Note: Fresh corn differs with the season. If the corn is watery when scraped and cut, add 2 tablespoons of flour to the corn before the rest of the ingredients are added.

Turnip Cups with Peas

Yields 12 servings

1 14½-ounce can chicken stock
12 small turnips, peeled
1 tablespoon lemon juice
1 10-ounce package frozen peas
1 tablespoon butter
1 tablespoon flour

Measure ½ cup chicken stock and set aside. Pour remaining stock into a large saucepan. Add turnips, lemon juice and enough water to cover. Simmer until turnips are tender but not too soft, about 15 minutes. Remove turnips with a slotted spoon and set aside to cool. Discard all but ½ cup liquid and add peas. Cook until done. Make a roux of butter, flour and reserved ½ cup stock. Add peas and set aside. Scoop out centers of turnips, leaving ¼- to ½-inch shells. Chop pulp and add to pea mixture; stuff into shells. Place in a well-buttered casserole and heat in 350° oven for 20 minutes.

Brussels Sprouts

Yields 12 servings

2 pounds Brussels sprouts
5 tablespoons butter, sliced
Salt and pepper to taste

Soak Brussels sprouts in salted cold water for 10 minutes. Remove and steam over boiling water for 5 minutes. Place in serving dish; add butter, salt and pepper; blend until butter is melted.

Dill Carrots

Yields 12 servings

2 pounds carrots, peeled and sliced
¼ cup fresh chopped dill or 1 tablespoon dried dill weed
4 tablespoons (½ stick) butter or margarine

Steam carrots in ¼ cup of water until tender. Drain; add dill and butter. Simmer for a few additional minutes.

Cranberry Salad

Yields 10 to 12 servings

2 3-ounce packages orange-flavored gelatin
1½ cups boiling water
2 teaspoons grated orange rind
1 16-ounce can cranberry sauce
1 8½-ounce can crushed pineapple, drained

½ cup diced celery
1 cup whole cranberries

Dissolve gelatin in boiling water; add orange rind and cranberry sauce. Stir until all dissolves. Chill until thickened; stir in pineapple, celery and cranberries. Pour into a 1½-quart mold and chill until firm.

Rockville Pears

Yields 4 to 5 pints

5 pounds very firm cooking pears
2 cups white vinegar
1½ cups water
5 cups sugar
6 sticks whole cinnamon, 2 inches long
1 tablespoon whole cloves
1 tablespoon whole allspice

Peel pears and cut into quarters. Put vinegar, water and sugar in a large saucepan. Tie spices together in cheesecloth and add to liquids. Bring all to a boil and cook 5 minutes. Add half the pears and cook until tender, approximately 10 minutes. Pack fruit in hot sterilized jars. Cook remaining fruit and fill remaining jars. Pour syrup over all the fruit in jars and seal.

Save the leftover syrup for making more pears. Syrup may be stored in the refrigerator. The cinnamon sticks can also be packed in the jars as decoration.

Miss Lucy's Yeast Rolls

Yields 4 dozen

1 cup shortening
¾ cup sugar
1 teaspoon salt
1 cup boiling water
2 packages yeast
1 cup warm water
2 eggs, beaten
6 cups flour
1 tablespoon butter, melted

Measure shortening, sugar and salt into a large mixing bowl. Add boiling water. Stir to dissolve sugar and set aside. Dissolve yeast in warm water in a small bowl. Set aside. Add beaten eggs to shortening mixture, then add yeast. Add flour, blending with electric mixer if desired. Cover bowl and refrigerate overnight. This dough may be stored several days. When ready to use, turn half of dough out onto a heavily floured board. Roll dough ¼ inch thick and cut into desired shapes. Place on greased pans, brush tops with melted butter, and cover with cloth; allow to rise for 1 hour or more at room temperature. Repeat with other half of dough, or store in refrigerator for later use. Preheat oven to 400°. When rolls have almost doubled in bulk, bake 10 to 12 minutes until browned. Rolls can be frozen.

Pumpkin Squares

Yields 12 to 15 squares

1¾ cup graham cracker crumbs
1⅓ cup sugar, divided
½ cup (1 stick) butter, melted
2 eggs, beaten
8 ounces cream cheese, softened
1 16-ounce can pumpkin
3 eggs, separated
½ cup milk
½ cup brown sugar
½ teaspoon salt
2 teaspoons cinnamon
½ teaspoon ginger
½ teaspoon ground nutmeg
¼ teaspoon ground cloves
1½ envelopes unflavored gelatin
1 cup whipping cream, whipped

Combine crumbs, ⅓ cup sugar and butter. Press into 9-by-13-inch pan. Blend 2 beaten eggs, ¾ cup sugar and cream cheese. Pour over crust and bake at 350° for 20 minutes. Mix pumpkin and 3 egg yolks with milk, brown sugar, salt and spices; cook in top of double boiler, stirring until thick. Soften gelatin in cold water and stir into hot mixture. Remove from heat. Beat egg whites with remaining ¼ cup sugar; fold into pumpkin mixture. Pour on top of cheese mixture. Chill until set; cut into squares and top with whipped cream. Garnish with Marzipan Pumpkins (see page 197).

Lane Cake

Yields 12 to 16 servings

4 White Cake Layers
Bourbon Nut Filling
Boiled Frosting
½ to ¾ cup large, perfect pecan halves

Place one layer of cake on serving platter. Divide Bourbon Nut Filling into fourths. Spread one-fourth of filling on top of layer. Repeat process three times. Ice sides with Boiled Frosting. Decorate with pecan halves.

WHITE CAKE LAYERS

1 cup (2 sticks) butter
2 cups sugar
3 cups sifted cake flour
1 tablespoon baking powder
¾ cup milk
1 teaspoon vanilla
8 egg whites, beaten until stiff peaks form

Cream butter and sugar together until light and fluffy. Combine flour and baking powder and add to creamed mixture alternately with milk. Stir in vanilla. Gently fold in beaten egg whites. Pour batter into 4 greased and floured 9-inch round pans. Bake at 350° for 15 to 18 minutes or until a cake tester comes out clean when inserted in middle. Cool in pans 10 minutes. Remove from pans to wire rack.

Cool completely. Layers tend to be fragile so handle carefully.

BOURBON NUT FILLING

8 egg yolks
2 cups sugar
1 cup (2 sticks) butter
2 cup chopped pecans
1 cup white raisins
½ cup good bourbon or brandy

In a heavy sauce pan, combine egg yolks, sugar and butter. Cook over low to medium heat until thickened, remove from heat and add pecans, raisins and bourbon. Cool.

BOILED FROSTING

1 cup sugar
3 tablespoons water
2 egg whites
Dash of salt
¼ teaspoon cream of tartar
1 teaspoon vanilla

Combine all ingredients, except vanilla, in top of double boiler. Before placing over hot water, beat one minute. Put over hot, but not boiling water and beat with electric mixer about 7 to 10 minutes or until frosting forms stiff peaks. Do not overcook. Stir in vanilla.

*Roast Turkey is the traditional main course for this Thanksgiving
celebration in the dining room of the Nathaniel Russell house.*

*Acorn Squash Soup is served from an early
nineteenth-century Chinese porcelain tureen.*

*Pumpkin Squares and Lane Cake amid antique
silver and glass on a Charleston-made sideboard.*

The main course of Roast Loin of Veal with Raspberry-Garlic Sauce is served around a magnificent nineteenth-century silver epergne standing on a mirrored plateau.

Baked Garlic with Feta Cheese at the Calhoun Mansion.

Mushroom Consommé flanked by Victorian repoussé flatware.

The velvety Princess Torte on a carved Empire sideboard.

Dinner at Eight
The Calhoun Mansion

THERE IS AN OLD SAYING about Charleston after the Civil War, suggesting that people were "too poor to paint and too proud to whitewash." For most, that was a truism in postbellum Charleston — but not for George W. Williams, who built one of the city's most imposing mansions between 1876 and 1878. Constructed at an estimated cost of $200,000, the building was described by a newspaper article in *The News and Courier* in 1876 as "probably the handsomest and most complete private residence in the South and one of the handsomest in this country."

Williams could easily have been the subject of a novel by Horatio Alger. As a young man, he arrived in Augusta, Georgia, with ten dollars in his pocket to join a wholesale grocery establishment. By age twenty-one, he was a partner in the firm, and at twenty-three, a director in the State Bank of Georgia. He moved to Charleston in 1852, where his company began importations of sugar and molasses from the West Indies, coffee from South America, and bagging from India, and soon his sales increased to two million dollars annually.

During the Civil War, the state legislature appointed Williams commissary to procure provisions for the soldiers' families. His largesse following the war must have been appreciated by the populace. The day after the city fell he "issued rations to some 10,000 people, all grades and colors from his private residence near Hampstead." Hav-

The border above is taken from a Drayton Hall overmantel detail.

ing saved stores of supplies from fire, he enabled 20,000 people to be fed for four months after the surrender of the city.

Following the war, Williams retained substantial capital and furthered his banking interests by putting much of his wealth in British pounds sterling. For his baronial mansion, George Williams secured the services of architect W. P. Russell. No expense was spared in the decoration of the thirty-five-room structure.

Through massive doors, one enters the foyer paved with imported encaustic tiles and paneled in walnut with satinwood inlay. A second pair of huge doors with glazed panels opens into the entrance hall which is fourteen feet wide, fourteen feet high and fifty feet long. There is a fireplace with English Minton tiles depicting Shakespeare's plays and a second-floor music room twenty-seven feet high with a walnut cornice and rope moldings set with heads of the Muses. The house is crowned with a cupola-cum-observatory affording panoramic views of the peninsular city.

In the dining room, the floors are inlaid with various woods; the walls are painted, stenciled, and gilded with stylized flowers and fleurs-de-lis. From the coffered ceiling, embellished with plaster panels of fruit clusters, hangs a bold bronze and brass gas chandelier. It is a room of high Victorian splendor demanding a menu of involved preparation and ceremonial presentation.

Following Williams' death, the property was acquired by his daughter and son-in-law, Patrick Calhoun, a grandson of John C. Calhoun. Recently, it has been lavishly restored by the present owner and is open to the public.

DINNER AT EIGHT

Serves 8

Kill the Chill Manhattan
Baked Garlic with Feta Cheese
Mushroom Consommé
Calhoun Mansion Oysters
Grand Marnier Sorbet
Onion Spiral Potatoes
Broccoli and Cauliflower with Rosemary Crumbs
Roast Loin of Veal with Raspberry-Garlic Sauce
Belgian Endive Salad
Princess Torte
Irish Creme Liqueur

Kill the Chill Manhattan

Yields 1 serving

2 ounces bourbon
1 ounce dry vermouth
2 dashes Angostura bitters
½ cup cracked ice
1 maraschino cherry

Add bourbon, vermouth and bitters to cracked ice and stir for a minute. Strain into serving glass and add cherry.

Baked Garlic
with Feta Cheese

Yields 8 servings

10 to 12 whole heads of garlic
2 tablespoons olive oil
Coarse salt
Freshly ground black pepper
⅓ to ½ pound feta cheese
4 ounces cream cheese, softened

Remove papery outer skin from the garlic heads, leaving the clusters of cloves intact. Arrange the heads in a baking dish large enough to hold them comfortably. Drizzle a few drops of olive oil on each cluster. Bake for 30 to 45 minutes at 350°, basting with oil every 15 to 20 minutes until garlic is tender and golden brown. Cool; using a sharp knife, remove the top of each garlic cluster. Season with salt and freshly ground pepper.

To serve: Mix together feta cheese and cream cheese and put in container. On large platter, arrange garlic clusters around the container of cheese mixture. Using a butter knife, spread a plain cracker with roasted garlic; top with feta cheese.

Mushroom Consommé

Yields 8 servings

¼ cup butter
½ cup chopped onion
¾ pound fresh mushrooms, sliced
1½ tablespoons lemon juice
2 cups hot water
2 beef bouillon cubes
2 cups beef broth
¼ teaspoon pepper
¼ cup vermouth
1 teaspoon sugar
Dash of nutmeg
Avocado for garnish

Melt butter and sauté onions until transparent. Add mushrooms and lemon juice and cook gently for 5 minutes. Add remaining ingredients and heat until just before boiling point. Garnish each serving with a slice of avocado.

Calhoun Mansion Oysters

Yields 8 servings

2 pints large oysters
½ of 10-ounce package fresh spinach
5 spring onions with greens
½ bunch fresh parsley
Top 3 inches of bunch of celery
   with green leaves
1 stick butter, cut into pieces

2 tablespoons Pernod
1 tablespoon Worcestershire sauce
3 tablespoons oyster juice
½ pound Parmesan cheese, freshly grated
   (may substitute Mozzarella)
Rock salt

Drain oysters and reserve juice. Put coarsely chopped spinach, onions, parsley and celery tops in food processor with steel blade and chop fine. Add butter and mix. Add Pernod, Worcestershire sauce and oyster juice and blend until well mixed. Mix ⅓ of the cheese into the mixture.

Place 4 to 5 oysters in each of 8 small ungreased gratin dishes. Cover with vegetable mixture. Sprinkle tops with remaining Parmesan cheese (additional grated Parmesan cheese may be added if desired). Set on baking sheets that have been filled with rock salt. Bake at 425° for about 5 minutes or until bubbly. Put under broiler for a few minutes until slightly browned on top.

Grand Marnier Sorbet
Yields 8 to 12 servings

½ cup sugar
1¾ cups water
¾ cup orange juice
¼ cup lemon juice
1 teaspoon grated orange rind
¼ cup Grand Marnier liqueur

Bring sugar and water to a boil and continue boiling for 5 minutes. Cool slightly. Add remaining ingredients and stir to blend. Cool, strain, and freeze overnight.

Onion Spiral Potatoes
Yields 8 servings

2 large single-bulb Bermuda onions
2 tablespoons butter or margarine
½ teaspoon salt
⅛ teaspoon pepper
4 cups mashed potatoes, seasoned to taste

Peel onions and slice crosswise into ½-inch slices. Place on jelly-roll pan 8 onion slices of equal size. Dot with butter and season with salt and pepper. Broil on one side for 6 minutes; turn and broil other side until tender but not mushy (4 minutes, watch carefully). On serving platter, make eight pyramid-style mounds of potatoes using an ice cream scoop. Place onion slice on top of each mound and gently pull outside rings down to create the spiral effect.

Broccoli and Cauliflower with Rosemary Crumbs
Yields 8 servings

1 head of cauliflower
1 bunch of broccoli
Rosemary Crumbs

Wash and core cauliflower. Cut into flowerettes. Repeat procedure for broccoli. In a vegetable steamer basket, arrange the broccoli and cauliflower in a mound, alternating green and white. Steam until tender—8 to 10 minutes. Remove to serving bowl; sprinkle with Rosemary Crumbs.

Continued . . .

ROSEMARY CRUMBS
7 tablespoons unsalted butter
1¾ cups fresh bread crumbs
1½ tablespoons dried parsley
½ teaspoon dried rosemary
Salt and pepper to taste

In a heavy skillet, melt butter over moderate heat. Add bread crumbs and cook, stirring often, until crumbs are golden brown. Add the herbs; season with salt and pepper to taste. Sprinkle over broccoli and cauliflower.

Roast Loin of Veal with Raspberry-Garlic Sauce
Yields 8 servings

4½-pound veal loin roast
3 tablespoons soy sauce
3 tablespoons lemon juice
3 tablespoons butter
1 teaspoon salt
1 teaspoon pepper
Raspberry-Garlic Sauce

Place roast in 325° oven. Cook for 25 minutes per pound (approximately 1 hour, 50 minutes for a 4½-pound roast). Combine soy sauce, lemon juice, butter, salt and pepper. After the first 30 minutes of roasting, baste roast with soy sauce mixture. Repeat every 30 minutes. Serve with Raspberry-Garlic Sauce.

RASPBERRY-GARLIC SAUCE
  Yields 1½ cups

12 ounces red raspberry jam (seedless)
2 cloves garlic, crushed

1 tablespoon lemon juice
1 tablespoon red wine vinegar
1 tablespoon port wine
Dash of salt
⅛ teaspoon freshly ground pepper

Place all ingredients in small saucepan and simmer for 15 minutes. Strain before serving.

Belgian Endive Salad
Yields 8 servings

1 pound Belgian endive (about 5 heads)
1 pound carrots
4 tablespoons minced parsley
½ cup salad oil
3 tablespoons vinegar
1 tablespoon Dijon mustard
½ clove garlic
Salt and pepper to taste

Separate endive into leaves, reserving 40 whole ones. Finely chop remaining endive. Grate carrots and toss with chopped endive and parsley. Mix remaining ingredients in a separate container and pour over vegetables. Arrange 5 whole endive leaves on each salad plate in a spoke pattern. In the center, spoon the carrot mixture.

Princess Torte
Yields 12 to 16 slices

2 Yellow Cake Layers
¾ cup Vanilla Custard

¾ cup raspberry preserves with
  or without seeds
1 cup heavy whipping cream, whipped
2 7-ounce packages marzipan roll
Green food coloring

Make cake according to directions on page 180. Cool completely. Freeze extra layer for later use. Cut layers in half horizontally to create four thin layers. To split layers evenly, insert toothpicks around layers to mark halfway point.

VANILLA CUSTARD
  Yields 1½ cups

¼ cup sugar
2½ tablespoons cornstarch
¼ teaspoon salt
1½ cups milk
1 egg
1½ teaspoons butter
¾ teaspoon vanilla

In a 3-quart saucepan, stir together sugar, cornstarch and salt. Using wire whisk, stir in milk. Cook over medium heat stirring constantly until mixture thickens and boils. Remove from heat; stir egg into a small amount of hot milk mixture. Slowly return egg mixture to hot milk mixture. Return to heat; cook, stirring constantly for 1 to 3 minutes. Add butter and vanilla; remove from heat. Chill for at least one hour before serving.

To assemble: Place layer of cake on cake stand with cut side facing up. Spread 3 to 4 tablespoons of raspberry preserves, then 3 to 4 tablespoons of Vanilla Custard, ending with 2 to 3 tablespoons of whipped cream. Spread preserves, custard and whipped cream to edge of cake. Repeat with another layer of cake, preserves, custard, and whipped cream. Continue until all 4 layers have been used. Do not put anything on top of the last layer.

Place marzipan in a small bowl; add a few drops of green food coloring. Work into dough gently until desired color is reached. Place dough between 2 large pieces of plastic wrap. Roll into large circle—marzipan needs to be very thin. Carefully remove one side of wrap (leave one side of plastic wrap in place until marzipan is in position). Gently cover cake with thin layer of marzipan, encircling entire cake. Refrigerate overnight; use cake within 24 hours.

Irish Creme Liqueur
Yields 1½ pints

1 cup Irish whiskey
1 14-ounce can sweetened condensed milk
4 eggs
2 tablespoons vanilla
2 tablespoons chocolate extract
1 tablespoon coconut extract
1 tablespoon instant coffee

In a blender, mix all ingredients together until thoroughly blended. Pour into a quart-size jar and refrigerate.

Oyster Roast
Drayton Hall

He was a bold man that first eat an oyster.
— Jonathan Swift

CHARLESTONIANS are glad he did. Oyster roasts are a popular entertainment in the Carolina Lowcountry: the homeliest of shellfish providing one of the tastiest repasts. William Butler's 1599 admonition, "It is unseasonable and unwholesome in all months that have not an 'r' in their name to eat an oyster," still holds true. Consequently, oyster roasts are given from September through April. While not unheard of within the city, oyster roasts are most popular in the country, closer to the estuaries where oyster beds thrive. Armed with shucking knives and gloves, diners work for their reward at a variety of oyster-centered events from political gatherings to fund-raising parties.

A favorite oyster roast venue is Drayton Hall plantation on the west bank of the Ashley River. Built between 1738 and 1742 for John Drayton, heir to some twenty rice, indigo and cotton plantations, Drayton Hall may have been the first truly Palladian villa in America. Published in Venice in 1570, Andrea Palladio's *I quattro libri dell' architettura* (Four Books of Architecture) was translated into English by Giacomo Leoni and published in London in 1716. Numerous examples of porticoes are illustrated. The Drayton Hall portico features Doric and Ionic columns of Portland stone imported from England. Open and airy, the portico would become a popular feature of buildings in Charleston and the surrounding Lowcountry.

Inside, the house again displays the importance of eighteenth-century European design books. The chimneypiece in the great room on the first floor is directly inspired by Plate 64 of William Kent's *Designs of Inigo Jones*, which was published in London in 1727. The fact that it was being used in the relative wilderness of Carolina scarcely a decade later is a credit to the style-consciousness of the Drayton family. And the Draytons apparently lived here in great style. The fastidious Duc de la Rochefoucauld-Liancourt visited in 1796 and noted, "We stopped to dine with Dr. Drayton at Drayton Hall. The house is an ancient building, but convenient and good; and the garden is better laid out, better cultivated and stocked with good trees, than any I have hitherto seen."

The house was occupied by seven generations of the Drayton family until 1974, but the family rarely felt the urge to update. Several delicate neoclassical mantels were added at the turn of the nineteenth century, and the window sashes were replaced after an 1813 hurricane blew out the original windows, which had twelve heavily mullioned panes in each sash. Even after the Draytons regained much of their wealth with the mining of phosphate, they cherished and maintained the house in all its eighteenth-century splendor.

One of the great glories of Drayton Hall is its remarkable state of preservation. The house has never been plumbed or wired and most of the rooms have only two coats of paint, the original and an 1870 update, leaving the extraordinary carving crisp and clean. The house was one of only three Ashley River plantations spared during the Civil War and remains today as the lone survivor. Untouched by well-intentioned restorers, Drayton Hall is shown daily by the National Trust for Historic Preservation as an architectural monument and one of the great treasures of Colonial American art.

OYSTER ROAST

Serves 50

Seasoned Popcorn
Roasted Oysters
Cocktail Sauce for Fifty   •   Drawn Butter
Fish Chowder
Lemon Pepper Crackers
Okra Soup
Chili
Lemon Poppy Seed Cake with Lemon Glaze
Prune Cake
Fudge Pound Cake with Chocolate Glaze
Apple Nut Cake with Cream Cheese Icing

Seasoned Popcorn

½ cup unpopped corn
  (1 quart popped corn)
1 tablespoon oil

In order for the seasoning to adhere, the popcorn must be popped in oil or sprayed with vegetable-oil baking spray after popping has ceased and while still warm.

SEASONING I
  Yields approximately 1 cup

3 tablespoons lemon pepper
½ cup dried basil leaves, crushed
1 tablespoon dried dill weed, crushed
2 tablespoons garlic powder
2 teaspoons salt

Mix ingredients together in food processor using steel blade. Sprinkle lightly on popcorn as soon as it is popped. Use ½ to 1 teaspoon per quart of popped corn.

SEASONING II
  Yields approximately 1 cup

1 cup freshly grated Parmesan cheese
1 tablespoon white pepper
1½ teaspoons paprika
1 teaspoon cumin

Mix ingredients together. Sprinkle lightly on popped corn. Use ½ to 1 teaspoon per quart of popped corn. This is a very spicy seasoning.

Roasted Oysters

The oyster roast is such a Southern tradition that most oyster lovers have their own cooking technique. Some roasts are very elaborate, with custom tables containing waste cans for empty shells, special equipment to steam the oysters, and an array of dipping sauces to please any palate. But a great feast and a great time can be had with this minimal amount of preparation and equipment.

10 bushels of oysters, rinsed of mud
  (1 bushel serves 5)
1 large sheet of metal—tin or steel,
  NOT aluminum
1 roaring fire, charcoal or wood
Several burlap bags, wet
Gloves or small towels
Oyster knives or screw drivers

When fire is going strong, prop the sheet of metal over the flames to create a flat cooking surface. Put oysters on top of metal sheet, one bushel at a time. Cover oysters completely with wet burlap bags. Bags may need to be resoaked between batches. Oysters are done when they pop open, but some like them slightly dried out, which requires an additional 5 minutes cooking time. With a large shovel, transfer oysters from fire to table. Insert knife in joint, pry open shell and remove oyster. Dip oyster in sauce and enjoy.

Cocktail Sauce
for Fifty
Yields 1½ quarts

1½ cups chili sauce
3 cups good tomato ketchup
1 tablespoon fresh lemon juice
2 tablespoons fresh parsley
5 ounces prepared horseradish, or more
  to taste
1 tablespoon Worcestershire sauce
¼ teaspoon salt
Pepper to taste
⅛ teaspoon Tabasco
Capers, optional

Mix above ingredients together. Chill until ready to serve.

Drawn Butter
Yields 2½ cups

6½ sticks butter

In a heavy saucepan, melt the butter over low heat. Remove the pan from the heat, let the butter stand for several minutes to allow the solids to settle to the bottom. Skim the clarified butter from the top and place in a container in the refrigerator until ready for use. Pour the clarified butter into a jar, cover, and store in the refrigerator. This will keep indefinitely. Clarified butter loses ¼ of its original volume. Reheat and keep warm in fondue pots and pour into small bowls as an accompaniment to the oysters.

Fish Chowder
Yields 25 servings

1¾ cups chopped onion
6 garlic cloves, minced
⅔ cup chopped green pepper
¼ cup olive oil
4 quarts Fish Stock
5 quarts peeled, finely diced potatoes
3 cups minced celery
6 bay leaves
2 tablespoons salt
2 teaspoons freshly ground white pepper
1 cup minced fresh parsley
6 cups any white fish, cooked and flaked

In a large pan, sauté onions, garlic and green peppers in olive oil until the onions are transparent. Add the Fish Stock, potatoes, celery, bay leaves, salt and pepper. Cook until the potatoes are tender. Just before serving, add the minced parsley and fish. Serve with Lemon Pepper Crackers. May be halved; freezes well.

FISH STOCK
  Yields approximately 1 gallon
6 pounds bones and trimmings of any
  white fish, such as sole or flounder
6 cups sliced onions
1½ cups parsley stems
⅔ cup lemon juice
2 teaspoons salt
2 cups dry white wine
4 quarts water

In a large saucepan, combine all ingredients. Bring to a boil, then reduce heat to a simmer, skimming froth. Cook for 25 minutes over moderate heat. Strain the stock through a fine sieve into a bowl, pressing liquid from the solids; cool. This may be frozen or used immediately for fish chowder.

Lemon Pepper Crackers

Yields 12 to 16 crackers

½ cup flour
1 teaspoon coarsely ground pepper
1 teaspoon grated lemon rind
2 tablespoons cold butter
1 tablespoon sour cream
1½ teaspoons lemon juice
Coarse salt for sprinkling on crackers

In a bowl with pastry cutter, blend the flour, pepper, rind and butter until mixture resembles meal; add the sour cream and lemon juice; toss the mixture gently—you may need to add ½ to 1 teaspoon of water—until it forms a dough. Shape dough into ball; wrap in plastic wrap and and chill for 30 minutes. On floured surface, roll dough ¹⁄₁₆ inch thick. Cut into rounds or your favorite shape. Place the rounds on ungreased baking sheet, sprinkle with coarse salt, and bake in a 400° oven for 12 minutes or until golden.

Note: Make 4 recipes to serve 25 people.

Okra Soup

Yields 25 servings

4 pounds chopped okra
4 28-ounce cans tomatoes
3 to 4 large onions, chopped
4 pounds stew beef
4 beef bouillon cubes
1½ quarts water
1 teaspoon sugar
1 teaspoon salt
1 teaspoon pepper

Brown beef in Dutch oven. Add remaining ingredients and simmer for 2 to 3 hours.

Chili

Yields 20 to 25 servings

4 cups chopped onions
2 cups chopped bell pepper
4 garlic cloves, minced
⅓ cup olive oil
3 28-ounce cans Italian plum tomatoes
    with juice
3 10¾-ounce cans tomato puree
2 15-ounce cans tomato sauce
2 16-ounce cans stewed tomatoes
¼ cup chili powder
½ tablespoon crushed red pepper flakes
3 tablespoons ground cumin
1 tablespoon hot chili powder, optional
1 tablespoon dried basil
1 tablespoon salt
2 pounds hot Italian sausage, cooked
    and drained

Continued . . .

3 pounds lean ground beef, cooked and
   drained
2 1-pound cans red kidney beans, drained

In a large kettle, cook the onions, peppers
and garlic in olive oil over moderately low
heat until the onions are transparent. Add
the tomatoes with juice, tomato puree,
stewed tomatoes and tomato sauce. Simmer for 15 minutes. Add the chili pow-
ders, red pepper flakes, cumin, basil, salt,
sausage and ground beef. Simmer the
chili for 1½ hours, stirring often. Stir in
the beans. This may be made several days
in advance and kept chilled or frozen.
Serve with sour cream, chopped green
onions, shredded sharp cheddar cheese
and chopped tomatoes as condiments, if
desired.

Lemon Poppy Seed Cake
with
Lemon Glaze
Yields 16 slices

1cup (2 sticks) butter at room temperature
2 cups sugar
3 eggs
3 cups flour
½ teaspoon baking soda
½ teaspoon salt
1 cup buttermilk
2 teaspoons dehydated lemon peel or
   2 tablespoons fresh lemon zest

¼ cup fresh lemon juice
¼ cup poppy seeds
Lemon Glaze

Grease and flour a 9-inch tube pan. Tap
out excess flour. Using an electric mixer,
beat the butter until it is fluffy and soft.
Add sugar; beat until it is well mixed.
Add eggs, one at a time, beating well after
each addition. Sift together the dry ingredients. Alternate adding small amounts of
dry ingredients and buttermilk, beating
after each addition. Stir in lemon peel,
fresh lemon juice and poppy seeds. Turn
into prepared pan and smooth the top.
Bake at 350° for 1 hour and 15 minutes
or until a cake tester gently inserted into
the middle comes out clean and dry.
Remove the cake from the oven and let it
stand for 5 minutes. Remove cake from
the pan and drizzle Lemon Glaze over the
top and sides.

LEMON GLAZE

¼ cup fresh lemon juice
⅓ cup sugar
2 tablespoons butter
1 teaspoon lemon peel

Over medium heat in a small saucepan,
combine the lemon juice, sugar, butter
and lemon peel. Bring to a boil. Remove
from heat; let stand until lukewarm. Gently drizzle warm glaze over Lemon Poppy
Seed Cake. Freezes well.

Prune Cake

Yields 16 slices

1½ cups white sugar
1 cup corn oil
3 eggs
3 cups flour
1 teaspoon soda
½ teaspoon cinnamon
½ teaspoon nutmeg
½ teaspoon salt
1 cup buttermilk
1 cup cooked, chopped prunes
1 teaspoon vanilla

Cream sugar and oil; add eggs one at time. Sift together dry ingredients. Continue beating as dry ingredients are added alternately with buttermilk. Fold in prunes and vanilla. Pour into ungreased tube or Bundt pan. Bake for 1 hour at 350°.

Fudge Pound Cake with Chocolate Glaze

Yields 16 slices

1 cup (2 sticks) butter, room temperature
2 cups sugar
4 eggs
8 ounces semisweet chocolate, melted
3 ounces unsweetened chocolate, melted
2 teaspoons vanilla
3 tablespoons brandy
2¼ cups flour
¼ teaspoon salt
1 teaspoon baking soda
1¼ cups buttermilk
Chocolate Glaze

In a large bowl, cream butter and sugar until light and fluffy. Add eggs, one at a time, beating well after each addition. Beat in chocolate, vanilla and brandy. Sift together dry ingredients. Add dry ingredients alternately with buttermilk. Pour mixture into greased and floured Bundt pan. Bake in center of preheated 350° oven for 1 hour or until a cake tester inserted in center comes out clean. Cool for 15 minutes. Remove from pan to cake plate. Pour Chocolate Glaze over the cake. It may be served with or without the glaze, or frozen without the glaze.

CHOCOLATE GLAZE

4 ounces semisweet chocolate
6 tablespoons butter
2 teaspoons light corn syrup

Melt chocolate and butter in double boiler. Remove from heat; stir in corn syrup and gently pour over cake.

Apple Nut Cake with Cream Cheese Icing

Yields 14 to 16 slices

2 cups sugar
3 eggs
1¼ cups vegetable oil
3 cups chopped raw apples

Continued . . .

1 cup chopped nuts
3 cups flour
1 teaspoon salt
1 teaspoon soda
2 teaspoons vanilla
Cream Cheese Icing

Beat eggs and sugar. Add oil, flour, salt, soda and vanilla; mix well. Stir in apples and nuts; the batter will be thick. Bake in three 9-inch layer cake pans at 325° for 45 to 50 minutes or in a tube pan for 1½ hours at 350°. Cool. Cake may be iced with Cream Cheese Icing or frozen prior to icing.

CREAM CHEESE ICING

½ cup (1 stick) butter, softened
8 ounces cream cheese, softened
1 box confectioners' sugar
1 teaspoon vanilla
½ cup chopped nuts

Cream the butter and cheese. Add the powdered sugar and vanilla. Stir in the nuts. This is very easy to make in a food processor, but be sure to stir in nuts by hand.

FACING PAGE

Roasted Oysters, Fish Chowder and Seasoned Popcorn await guests under a live oak at Drayton Hall, America's premier Palladian house.

Curried Shrimp with Rice, Artichoke Bottoms Stuffed with Spinach and Tossed Salad Delmonico are the main course for a supper club buffet at the Thomas Rose house.

Gouda Cheese in Puff Pastry and Confetti Spread served with Frozen Whiskey Sours.

Coconut Cake and Banana Cake presented beside nineteenth-century silver candlesticks.

Supper Club Dinner
The Thomas Rose House

WHILE MOST FREQUENTLY CHRONICLED by visitors to the city, Charleston's legendary hospitality also extends to one's friends and neighbors. On a monthly basis, a variety of supper clubs meet to enjoy good food, wine and conversation. Members share in the preparation of the meal on a rotating scheme and menus range from simple picnic buffets to more elaborately conceived banquets. Supper club dinners provide the perfect time to catch up with friends and try out new recipes.

The setting for this supper club feast is the dining room of the Thomas Rose house, one of Charleston's earliest and best-preserved dwellings. In 1733, wealthy Irishman Thomas Rose married Beuler Elliott, the youngest of Thomas Elliott's eighteen children. Elliott's success as a rice planter enabled him to provide a substantial inheritance for all of his children: to each son, he left a plantation; to each daughter, a property in town.

While an exact date has not been assigned, the handsome early-Georgian house was obviously built by the Roses sometime between 1734 and 1740. It shows up on a plot of the city as one of the houses that survived the devastating fire of November 18, 1740, in which an estimated 300 houses were consumed. A letter recently discovered in Belfast, Ireland, confirms that Thomas Rose wrote in 1734 asking his Irish family to locate four workmen willing to come to Carolina to work for him, presumably on this house.

The floor plan is representative of Charleston's early houses of substance, with an asymmetrical arrangement allowing for a grand second-floor drawing room or "hall," as it would have been called in the eighteenth century. This is reached by way of an enclosed stair hall or passage to the side of the house, the stair itself featuring turned balusters and carved brackets of rich black walnut. Throughout the house, the bold raised panel Georgian woodwork is almost as Thomas Rose knew it, the minor changes being confined to neoclassical mantels added in an effort to update about 1800.

Restored with meticulous care in the 1940's, the Thomas Rose house is appointed with an enviable collection of furnishings from the eighteenth and early nineteenth centuries. The dining room is at the back of the house, its windows overlooking the piazza and the splendid garden planned and developed by landscape architect Loutrel Briggs in 1954–1955. Painted in two subtle shades of green, the paneling is original except the Federal mantel and cupboard surrounds, which now house a portion of the collection of American birds and flowers designed by Dorothy Doughty for Royal Worcester between 1935 and 1962.

A portrait of a lady above the mantel is attributed to Benjamin West, the American Quaker who expatriated to London where he would eventually enjoy royal patronage. The first American artist of international reputation, West succeeded Sir Joshua Reynolds as president of the Royal Academy in 1792. Flanking the portrait are two English lead chestnut urns from the late eighteenth century, originally used to transport hot roasted chestnuts from the hearth to the table.

SUPPER CLUB

Serves 20

Frozen Whiskey Sours
Confetti Spread
Gouda in Puff Pastry with Horseradish Sauce
Curried Shrimp with Rice
Artichoke Bottoms Stuffed with Spinach
Tossed Salad Delmonico
Mama Jo's Cornmeal Rolls
Coconut Cake
Banana Cake

Frozen Whiskey Sours

Yields 15 cups

1 12-ounce can frozen orange juice
1 12-ounce can frozen limeade
1 12-ounce can frozen lemonade
2 tablespoons lemon juice
6 cups water
5 cups bourbon

Thaw juices and transfer to a large bowl. Add water and bourbon and stir until well blended. Freeze in two half-gallon containers. Mixture will remain slightly slushy and will keep for several months. To serve frozen, scoop mixture into glass, add a few drops of water and stir to liquefy. To serve on the rocks, thaw mixture and pour over ice.

Confetti Spread

Yields 15 to 20 servings

8 ounces cream cheese, softened
2 tablespoons milk
1 2½-ounce jar of chipped beef,
   cut into small pieces
2 tablespoons minced onion
2 tablespoons chopped green pepper
½ teaspoon pepper
½ cup sour cream
¼ cup coarsely chopped walnuts
Assorted crackers

Blend cream cheese and milk. Stir in dried beef, onion, green pepper and pepper. Mix well. Stir in sour cream. Spoon into 8-inch pie plate or baking dish.

Sprinkle walnuts on top. Bake at 350° for 15 minutes. Serve hot with crackers.

Gouda in Puff Pastry with Horseradish Sauce

Yields 10 servings

1 6½-ounce round of Gouda cheese,
   red rind removed
6-inch square of puff pastry

Center Gouda on square of puff pastry. Bring sides up and together. Seal edges; top may be decorated if desired. Bake in a 350° oven for 45 minutes or until golden brown. Serve with crackers, apple and pear slices, and Horseradish Sauce. Make two recipes for 20 servings.

HORSERADISH SAUCE

Yields 1⅓ cups

1 cup sour cream
2 tablespoons prepared horseradish
2 tablespoons fresh parsley, minced
⅓ cup half-and-half

Mix all ingredients thoroughly. Pour into small dish and refrigerate until ready to serve. This may also be used with red meats.

Curried Shrimp with Rice

Yields 10 to 12 servings

3 cups raw rice
1 medium onion, chopped

1 cup (2 sticks) butter
2 teaspoons curry powder
2 teaspoons pepper
1 teaspoon salt
5 pounds shrimp, cooked and cleaned
1 cup chopped pecans
1½ cups raisins
12 slices bacon, cooked and crumbled

Cook rice. Sauté onion in butter; add curry, pepper and salt. Combine onion mixture, rice, shrimp, pecans and raisins. Place in casserole and heat for 20 minutes at 350°. Before serving, sprinkle with bacon. Recipe may be halved; make 1½ recipes to serve 20. Freezes well; be sure to thaw in refrigerator.

Artichoke Bottoms Stuffed with Spinach
Yields approximately 21

2 10-ounce packages frozen chopped
   spinach
½ cup minced onion
6 tablespoons butter
4+ tablespoons Parmesan cheese
½ cup sour cream
Salt and pepper to taste
Dash of cayenne
3 14-ounce cans artichoke bottoms

Cook spinach according to directions; drain. Sauté onions in butter until tender. Stir in spinach, sour cream, Parmesan cheese, salt and pepper. Spoon mixture into artichoke bottoms. Place in shallow baking dish and sprinkle with more Parmesan. Add water to barely cover bottom of dish. Bake at 350° for 20 minutes. This recipe may also be made with yellow squash. Blanch squash halves and remove pulp to form shell for stuffing.

Tossed Salad Delmonico
Yields 20 servings

3 to 4 heads lettuce, mixed varieties
1 cup olive oil
⅓ cup wine vinegar
⅓ cup cream
4 ounces Roquefort cheese
Freshly ground black pepper
Dash of hot pepper sauce
4 hard-cooked eggs, finely chopped
4 slices bacon, cooked and crumbled

Wash and dry lettuce. Allow to crisp in refrigerator. Combine oil, vinegar, cream and Roquefort in small bowl. Add pepper and hot sauce, whisking until smooth. Stir in chopped egg and crumbled bacon. At serving time, arrange lettuce in large bowl, pour dressing over, toss and serve.

Mama Jo's Cornmeal Rolls
Yields 2 dozen

⅓ cup corn meal
½ cup sugar
1 teaspoon salt
½ cup (1 stick) butter
2 cups milk

Continued . . .

1 package yeast
¼ cup warm water
2 eggs
4 cups flour, or more
Melted butter for tops

Combine the cornmeal, sugar, salt, butter and milk in a large saucepan. Cook over medium heat until thick. Set aside and let cool. In a small bowl, dissolve yeast in water. Add yeast mixture to cooled cornmeal mixture. Add eggs and 2 cups flour. Beat mixture thoroughly. Add rest of flour. Form dough into ball. Coat with small amount of butter. Cover and let rise 2 hours or until doubled in bulk. Punch down. Turn dough onto floured board. Form into shapes of your choice. Lightly coat tops with butter. Let rise 1 hour. Bake at 350° in greased tins or pans for 15 minutes, or until top is golden brown. Cooked rolls may be frozen for later use.

Coconut Cake
Yields 16 slices

3 Yellow Cake Layers
Sour Cream Coconut Filling
Boiled Frosting
1 cup grated coconut, fresh or frozen

Place one cake layer on serving platter. Cover with ¼ to ½ cup of sour cream filling. Add second layer, cover with ¼ to ½ cup of Sour Cream Coconut Filling. Top with third layer and cover with remaining sour cream mixture. Cake may be served at this stage if desired. To serve as pic-tured in book, frost top and sides with Boiled Frosting (see page 154). Press coconut on sides of cake. Flavor is best if made one to two days ahead. Refrigerate until ready to serve.

YELLOW CAKE LAYERS
  Yields 3 cake layers

1 cup (2 sticks) butter
2 cups sugar
4 eggs
3 cups sifted cake flour
1 tablespoon baking powder
¼ teaspoon salt
1 cup milk
1 teaspoon vanilla

Cream butter; gradually add sugar, beating mixture until light and fluffy. Add eggs, one at a time, beating well after each addition. Combine flour, baking powder and salt. Add to creamed mixture, alternately with milk, until thoroughly mixed. Stir in vanilla. Pour batter into 3 greased and floured 9-inch round pans. Bake at 350° for 20 to 25 minutes or until a cake tester comes out clean when inserted in the middle. Cool in pans 10 minutes; remove from pans and cool completely.

SOUR CREAM COCONUT FILLING

1½ cups sour cream
4 cups shredded or grated coconut, fresh or frozen
¾ cup confectioners' sugar
1 to 1½ teaspoons vanilla

Mix ingredients together in a large bowl. Stir until thoroughly blended.

Banana Cake

Yields 16 servings

½ cup (1 stick) butter
1½ cups sugar
2 eggs
1¼ cups mashed overripe bananas
2 cups flour
¼ teaspoon salt
¾ teaspoon baking soda
½ teaspoon baking powder
¼ cup buttermilk
1½ teaspoons vanilla extract
2 to 3 bananas, sliced in ¼-inch slices
¼ cup orange juice
2 cups hazelnuts, finely chopped
12 whole hazelnuts
Cream Cheese Icing (see page 172)

Preheat oven to 350°. Grease and flour two 9-inch layer cake pans. Cream butter and sugar until light and fluffy. Add eggs and beat thoroughly. Add mashed bananas, blending well. Sift dry ingredients together and add one third at a time. Mix until blended. Stir in buttermilk and vanilla. Pour batter into prepared pans. Bake for 25 to 30 minutes or until a cake tester comes out clean when inserted in the middle. Cool in pans 5 minutes. Unmold and place on rack until thoroughly cool. The layers are moist, about 1 inch thick; they may be frozen.

To frost: Place one cake layer on cake stand. Cover layer with Cream Cheese Icing. Cover layer with sliced bananas that have been dipped in orange juice and drained. Cover with second layer. Ice entire cake, top and sides. Cut a piece of waxed paper to cover area between cake and stand. Press chopped hazelnuts into sides of cake. Remove excess nuts and waxed paper. Keep extra slices of banana in orange juice until ready to serve cake. When ready to serve, drain banana slices thoroughly. Place 12 slices on outer rim of cake. Top each slice of banana with a whole hazelnut. This cake will not keep more than 2 days.

Christmas Dinner
The Joseph Manigault House

OUR CULINARY YEAR comes to an end with a festive Christmas dinner in the splendid dining room of the Joseph Manigault house, completed about 1803 and now a property of the Charleston Museum. Christmas in Charleston during the eighteenth and early nineteenth centuries was a holy day when services were held in local parish churches and the sacrament was given. Traditionally, slaves and laborers were exempted from work, but otherwise the season was associated with little of the pomp celebrated today. In fact, December was generally regarded as a dull season in Charleston. Writing in 1786, Joseph Manigault complained of the lack of activity in December:

> It is as unfashionable to be here at this season, as in London in summer. You meet nobody but shopkeepers and tradesmen. I am heartily tired of their vulgar countenances, and it is probably I may come in the country for a day or two by way of recreation.

English traveler Tyrone Power found a similar situation in 1834.

> At this season Charleston is dull to a proverb, most of the planters, with their families, being in the country, and the rest preparing to follow; the city is, therefore, nearly abandoned to the cotton-shippers; and so it will remain until the month of February, when the race-meeting draws the

> whole State together; and, for a period of four or five weeks, few places,
> as I learn, can be more lively or more sociable.

The custom of hearty eating and drinking and general good cheer during the Christmas season did pervade early Charleston, whether in town or on the plantation. Had Mr. Manigault remained in the city, he might have enjoyed a bounteous feast such as this in the house designed for him by his brother, accomplished amateur architect Gabriel Manigault.

Gabriel Manigault was a fourth-generation Charlestonian, his great-grandfather Pierre having come to Carolina from France with other Huguenots in the late seventeenth century. The son of vastly wealthy planter Peter Manigault, who owned the finest library in colonial Charleston, Gabriel enjoyed the advantages of a superior education. Like many sons of Charleston's Huguenot oligarchs, Gabriel was sent to Geneva for schooling, after which he traveled widely in Europe, eventually ending up in London where he read law. His European experience must have kindled his love for architecture and he is generally credited with introducing the full-blown Adamesque or Federal style to Charleston. Charleston's city hall (originally the Bank of the United States) and South Carolina Society Hall attest to his considerable design skills. Sadly, one of his most accomplished buildings, the chapel of the Charleston Orphan House of 1802, was demolished in the 1950's despite the protests of preservationists, to make way for a parking lot.

The house Gabriel Manigault designed for his brother Joseph is entered through a garden lodge in the form of a temple. Of three full stories, an impressive stair hall features a spiral stair set in a half-round projection on the north side of the house. This neoclassical taste for curvilinear shapes is repeated in the elliptical double piazza, which balances the projecting apsidal end of the dining room on the opposite side.

Here, delicate composition plasterwork adorns the cornice and mantel providing an appropriate setting for an enviable collection of decorative arts of the early nineteenth century, made or owned by Charlestonians. The magnificent English Regency silver centerpiece by silversmith Paul Storr is filled with fruit crowned by a pineapple, a traditional symbol of hospitality. Even the most world-weary planter could be lured back to town from the country to enjoy such a Christmas holiday feast.

CHRISTMAS DINNER

Serves 16

Charleston Egg Nog
Stuffed Celery • Tomato Aspic
Baked Ham with Crunchy Topping
Roast Venison Haunch • Roast Turkey *
Sweet Potatoes in Orange Cups
Broccoli with Caper Sauce
Oyster Pie • Potato Stuffing
Auntie's Artichoke Relish • Pickled Peaches
Brandied Cranberries • Miss Lucy's Yeast Rolls**
Tropical Ambrosia • Wine Jelly with Boiled Custard
Fruit Cake Squares
Mincemeat Pie with Hard Sauce

* See page 149.   ** See page 153.

Charleston Egg Nog

Yields 48 servings

18 eggs
2½ cups sugar
½ cup brown sugar
1½ cups Barbados rum
1 quart bourbon
2 tablespoons vanilla
2 quarts milk
6 cups half-and-half
1½ cups whipping cream
Nutmeg, optional

Separate eggs. Beat yolks well, gradually adding sugars. Mix rum, bourbon and vanilla. Add slowly to egg-yolk mixture while continuously stirring. Next, add milk and half-and-half; continue stirring. Beat egg whites until stiff; fold into mixture. Whip cream and add. Serve in punch cups; top with freshly grated nutmeg.

Stuffed Celery

Yields 24 servings

4 ounces pimentos with liquid
12 ounces medium sharp Cheddar cheese, shredded
½ cup Miracle Whip Salad Dressing
½ teaspoon onion salt, optional
8 stalks of celery, each cut into thirds
¼ cup chopped nuts, optional

Mash pimentos, even if they are diced. Combine shredded cheese, pimentos, liquid and salad dressing. Add onion salt if desired. Stuff celery and sprinkle with nuts if desired. The consistency is intentionally thick for stuffing the celery. To thin for sandwiches add ¼ cup more salad dressing.

Tomato Aspic

Yields 16 servings

4 envelopes unflavored gelatin
1 cup cold water
4 cups V-8 Juice
¼ cup vinegar
½ cup chopped onion
½ teaspoon salt
½ teaspoon pepper
2 cups chopped celery
1 cup chopped green pepper
2 cups chopped olives, green or black
2 tablespoons lemon juice

Sprinkle gelatin into cold water; set aside. Bring juice, vinegar, onion, salt and pepper to a boil in a 2-quart saucepan. Remove from heat. Add softened gelatin and stir to dissolve. Add celery, green pepper, olives and lemon juice. Pour into a lightly greased 8-cup mold or 16 individual molds. Chill for several hours before serving. Recipe may be halved.

Baked Ham
with Crunchy Topping

Yields 16 servings

1 10- to 12-pound smoked ham
1 cup fine, dry bread crumbs

Continued . . .

1 cup brown sugar
¼ cup juice from spiced peaches
   (or any fruit juice)
1 teaspoon prepared mustard
½ teaspoon dry mustard
Whole cloves

Bake smoked ham as usual—uncovered, 25 to 30 minutes per pound at 325°. If desired, baste with fruit juice. When one hour of cooking time remains, remove ham from oven, turn heat to 400°. Make a paste by mixing bread crumbs, brown sugar, peach juice and mustards. Cut away skin. Make diagonal criss-cross gashes in the fatty layer. Spread paste over ham and rescore gashes if necessary. Put a clove in the center of each diamond and return ham to oven for last hour of baking at 400°. Best when sliced paper-thin.

Roast Venison Haunch

Yields 16 small servings

1 6- to 8-pound vension haunch,
   trimmed of excess fat
1 teaspoon or more pepper
8 to 10 strips bacon

Accurately weigh haunch that is ready to roast. Preheat oven to 500°. Pepper the roast very generously and rub into meat with hands. Place roast in pan and wrap all exposed meat with one layer of bacon strips. Cook in 500° oven 5 minutes per pound. Timing is the same with or without the bone. DO NOT OPEN OVEN. When allotted time is up, turn off oven but leave roast in oven for at least one more hour. (It may be left in for several hours.) Remove bacon before serving; use it to flavor rice or another dish. Garnish with purple grapes and parsley.

This method of cooking should not be used if the deer has been run by dogs.

Sweet Potatoes in Orange Cups

Yields 16 servings

8 oranges
8 cups cooked and mashed sweet potatoes
1 stick butter
¾ cup brown sugar
1 teaspoon grated orange or lemon rind
1 teaspoon salt
16 marshmallows

Halve the oranges and scoop out the pulp, saving rinds. Make zig-zags or scallops around the top edges of rinds. Mix orange juice and pulp with all other ingredients, except marshmallows. Pack mixture into the hollow rinds and place in a baking pan. Cover the dish closely; may be frozen at this point. If frozen, thaw at room temperature before baking. Preheat oven to 375°. Bake for 15 minutes. Remove cover and bake until brown. At last minute, top each with a marshmallow and return to heat until marshmallow melts and browns.

Broccoli with Caper Sauce

Yields 16 servings

3 bunches broccoli
1½ cups mayonnaise
3 tablespoons fresh tarragon chopped, or
   2 teaspoons dried
3 tablespoons chopped parsley
1 large clove garlic, minced
1½ teaspoons dry mustard
4½ teaspoons capers
4½ teaspoons chopped pickle
   of your choice

Steam broccoli until crisp-tender. Combine remaining ingredients for sauce and warm over very low heat. At serving time, pour sauce over broccoli.

Oyster Pie

Yields 14 to 16 small servings

1 quart large oysters, drained
2 tablespoons prepared horseradish
Salt and pepper to taste
2 rolls Ritz Crackers, each roll crushed
   separately
1 to 1½ cup half-and-half
6 tablespoons butter

In a 9-by-12-inch baking dish, make a layer using half of the oysters. Daub each oyster with horseradish. Season with salt and pepper, being generous with the pepper. Top with half of the cracker crumbs. Repeat the layer ending with dots of butter on top of the cracker crumbs. Pour half-and-half over to cover. Bake at 350° for 45 minutes.

Potato Stuffing

Yields 16 servings

10 medium potatoes, peeled and quartered
1¼ pounds bacon, finely chopped
2 large onions, chopped
2 large bell peppers, chopped
4 stalks of celery, chopped
Salt and pepper to taste

Cook potatoes until tender. Fry bacon, add onion, bell pepper and celery; sauté until onion is transparent. Mash potatoes and add the bacon mixture, including drippings. Salt and pepper to taste. Stuff turkey or bake as a side dish at 350° for 30 minutes. This recipe will stuff a 20-pound turkey; bake any remaining stuffing in a casserole dish at 350° for 30 minutes.

Auntie's Artichoke Relish

Yields 20 pints

1 peck Jerusalem artichokes
5 pounds onions
8 bell peppers
5 pounds cabbage
2¼ cups salt
2½ cups flour
1 1-ounce box turmeric
1 2-ounce box dry mustard
1½ gallons vinegar

Continued . . .

1   1⅛-ounce box celery seed
1   1¾-ounce box mustard seed
2 cups sugar

Clean artichokes and slice. Slice onions and bell peppers. Shred cabbage. Put these together in a large container and sprinkle with 2 cups salt. Let stand overnight. Next morning, squeeze all juice out of artichoke mixture. Mix together flour, mustard and turmeric. Warm ½ gallon vinegar and gradually add to the turmeric mixture to make a roux.

Divide the roux into two large pots. Bring to a boil. Divide between pots the celery seed, mustard seed, sugar and remaining salt; bring to a boil again, stirring occasionally. Divide vegetables into each pot and bring to a boil, stirring occasionally. Pour into sterilized jars and top loosely with lids. After one hour, screw lids on as tightly as possible.

Pickled Peaches
Yields 8 quarts

*8 pounds peaches (approximately 30
   to 32, small)*
3 pounds (6 cups) sugar, white or brown
3 cups cider vinegar
3 to 4 cinnamon sticks
1 to 2 tablespoons whole cloves

Peel peaches. Stick 3 cloves into each peach. Make a syrup with the sugar, vinegar and 2 of the cinnamon sticks by cooking them together for 15 minutes. Add as many of the peaches as possible; cook until tender, approximately 6 minutes. Using a slotted spoon, fill jars with peaches. Continue cooking until all peaches are done. Pour syrup into each jar, covering peaches; seal and process in a water bath. Bring water to a boil in a canner or large pan. Have level of water deep enough to reach top of jars. Use a rack on the bottom to keep jars from cracking. Lower jars into water, making sure they don't touch, and allow to process for 20 minutes. Carefully remove jars, using tongs, to a wooden or cloth-covered surface for cooling.

Brandied Cranberries
Yields 3 cups

12 ounces fresh cranberries
1½ cups sugar
1 cup water
3 to 5 whole cloves
2 whole allspice
1 cinnamon stick
2 tablespoons brandy

Wash berries; remove stems and over-soft berries. In large saucepan, combine berries, sugar, water and spices; bring to a boil. Reduce heat and simmer about 10 minutes, stirring occasionally. Add brandy and allow to simmer another 3 minutes. Remove from heat and pour into three 8-ounce jars or suitable containers for your serving needs. Store in refrigerator up to one month.

Tropical Ambrosia
Yields 16 servings

16 oranges, peeled and sliced crosswise
1 cup chopped dates
1 cup grated coconut
Juice of 2 fresh oranges

Mix the oranges, dates, coconut and juice together and chill 6 or more hours. (Prepackaged chopped dates dusted with dextrose stay soft and tender.)

Wine Jelly
with Boiled Custard
Yields 16 servings

4½ tablespoons unflavored gelatin
1 cup cold water
3⅓ cups boiling water
2 cups sugar
⅔ cup orange juice
6 tablespoons lemon juice
2 cups port wine
Boiled Custard

Soak gelatin 5 minutes in cold water; dissolve in boiling water. Add sugar, fruit juices and wine. Strain. Chill in a medium bowl and scoop into sherbets after congealed. Serve with Boiled Custard. Recipe may be halved.

BOILED CUSTARD
   Yields 2⅓ cups

2 eggs
4 tablespoons sugar

Pinch of salt
2 cups milk
1 teaspoon vanilla

Beat eggs; add sugar and salt and mix well. Add milk and blend. Cook in top of double boiler over medium heat until mixture coats spoon. Stir constantly and do not allow to boil. Let cool and add vanilla. Chill. Serve 1 to 2 tablespoons over Wine Jelly.

Fruit Cake Squares
Yields 28

CRUST

½ cup (1 stick) butter
¼ cup sugar
1 egg
1¼ cups sifted plain flour
⅛ teaspoon salt

Cream butter and sugar; add egg and beat well. Add flour and salt to mixture. Spread dough evenly over greased 9-by-13-inch pan. Bake at 325° for 10 minutes. Top with Fruit Topping and Glaze. These may be frozen or stored in tightly covered tins for several weeks.

FRUIT TOPPING

2 eggs, well beaten
1½ cups light brown sugar
¼ cup chopped pecans
½ cup chopped dates
½ cup coconut
½ cup candied pineapple

Continued . . .

½ cup candied cherries
½ teaspoon baking powder
½ teaspoon salt
2 tablespoons flour
1 teaspoon vanilla

Combine all ingredients, mix well and spread over baked crust. Return to 325° oven and bake 18 to 20 minutes longer. Remove from oven and let cool. Top with Glaze.

GLAZE

1½ cups confectioners' sugar
3 tablespoons lemon juice

Mix powdered sugar with lemon juice. Drizzle in a thin stream over baked squares in a criss-cross fashion.

Mincemeat Pie
with Hard Sauce

Yields 8 to 10 servings

1 28-ounce jar ready-to-use mincemeat
1 large apple, cored and diced
1 cup coarsely chopped walnuts
½ cup brown sugar
¼ cup brandy or rum
1 tablespoon lemon juice
Cream Cheese Pastry
Hard Sauce

Stir together the mincemeat, apple, walnuts, brown sugar, brandy and lemon juice until well mixed. Set aside. Prepare pastry; line 9-inch pie plate. Preheat oven to 425°. Spoon undrained mincemeat mixture into Cream Cheese Pastry pie crust. Cover with top crust. Bake 30 to 40 minutes until golden. Cool on wire rack 1 hour. Serve warm with Hard Sauce.

CREAM CHEESE PASTRY
Yields one bottom and top crust

8 ounces cream cheese, softened
2 cups flour
1 cup (2 sticks) butter, softened

Mix ingredients together in a food processor until dough forms a ball; wrap and chill for at least 12 hours. Divide dough in half. Turn dough on floured surface. Using a rolling pin, roll dough from center out. Roll to ⅛-inch thickness. Line 9-inch pie pan with dough. Prick bottom and sides of pastry. Prepare top crust in same manner. Use scraps to make holiday designs to decorate the top crust.

HARD SAUCE
Yields enough for 1 to 2 pies

¼ cup (½ stick) butter, softened.
1½ cups confectioners' sugar
½ teaspoon vanilla extract
1 tablespoon brandy

Cream sugar and butter; add vanilla and brandy. Mixture will be pliable like cookie dough. Shape into rolls 2 or 3 inches in diameter; wrap in foil and refrigerate. Let sit at room temperature 20 minutes to soften before slicing. Hard Sauce may be frozen.

A bounteous Christmas holiday feast is served on a Chinese-export Fitzhugh dinner service in the dining room of the Joseph Manigault house.

The dessert course of Tropical Ambrosia, Wine Jelly with Boiled Custard, Mincemeat Pie with Hard Sauce and Fruit Cake Squares.

A Baked Ham with Crunchy Topping awaits carving on Christmas day.

Pickled Peaches, Brandied Cranberries and Auntie's Artichoke Relish.

Venison garnished with apricots and grapes delights the eye.

Creative Garnishing

PRESENTING FOOD in a pleasing manner and to its best advantage is truly an art. Creating a work of art with eye appeal can make even a mundane food unforgettable.

Garnishes add that extra touch that appeals to the senses, giving food flair and pizazz. They are used to enhance, not to mask, the appearance of foods. Garnishes should be edible, and should add a new dimension to the food they decorate.

The garnishing ideas presented are easy and basic and will add color, texture and contrast to most dishes. Use your creativity; try new and different ideas. Only your imagination will limit you.

Following are some hints to insure success:

1. Plan ahead. Allow ample time for preparation. For best results, most of the garnishes shown here should be soaked in ice water overnight.

2. Be patient. Read and follow all directions, take your time, and be prepared to make extras.

3. Have plenty of ice on hand. Ice preserves garnishes and allows them to be kept for one week or longer.

4. Proper equipment is essential. Knives should be sharp and free of rust. Use these tools only for preparing garnishes. Wrap knives in paper towels to prevent nicking, and store in a drawer or cardboard box.

5. A knife sharpener is a must.

6. Select fruits and vegetables that are uniform in shape and free of blemishes and bruises.

7. It is easier to work with vegetables and fruits at room temperature, especially the root vegetables.

8. To make vegetables pliable, soak slices in two cups of water to which salt has been added. Soak ten minutes or until vegetables are soft. Vegetables can also be blanched to make them easier to work with.

9. Lemon juice is a must—fresh, frozen, or reconstituted. Lemon juice prevents fruits from darkening and removes odors from hands. (An emergency substitute can be made by crushing two vitamin C tablets in one cup of water.)

10. Unflavored gelatin can be used to coat fruits, vegetables and meats to preserve them and make them shine. Use one-half package of unflavored gelatin in one-half cup of cold water. Heat for one minute in the microwave and allow to cool. Using a pastry brush, coat each item with liquid gelatin and refrigerate until ready to use.

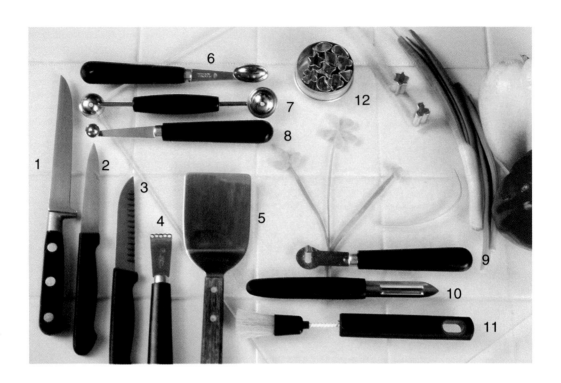

The Tools of Garnishing

1. 4-inch paring knife
2. 2½-inch paring knife
3. Serrated knife
4. Zester
5. Straight-edged metal spatula
6. Oval melon baller
7. Dual-sized melon baller
8. Tiny Parisian scoop
9. Zesteur
10. Swivel-bladed vegetable peeler
11. Pastry brush
12. Fancy aspic cutters

Watermelon, Cantaloupe or Honeydew Basket

Select a melon that is oval in shape and blemish-free. Cut a thin slice from the bottom to create a stable base.

Using an ice pick or pencil, draw the lines of the basket on the skin before starting to cut. The handle on a watermelon should be 3

to 4 inches wide; on small melons, 2 to 3 inches wide. Sawtoothed or scalloped designs can be used around the edges. Be careful not to cut through the handle.

Carefully lift sections on each side of the handle away; these can be used for other garnishes. Use a knife or melon baller to remove the pulp of the melon from the rind. Leave 1

to 1½ inches of rind intact. Fill the melon with fruits of your choice. If desired, decorate the handle with melon balls of a contrasting color, maraschino cherries, grapes, or tiny flowers made with aspic cutters.

Shrimp Boat

To create a stable base, cut a lengthwise slice ¼ inch thick from one side of a large cucumber; discard the slice. On the top side, make a slice ¼ inch thick approximately three-fourths of the length of the cucumber; do not cut the slice completely away. Carefully lift the top slice and secure it with a wooden skewer to create a mast. Form a flag with a thin, triangular slice of beet, carrot or turnip;

thread onto the skewer. Attach as shown.

Hollow out the inside with a knife or melon baller. Fill with shrimp.

Chocolate Curls

Melt 4 4-ounce bars of semisweet chocolate in the top of a double boiler over simmering

water. Stir occasionally until melted. Spoon melted chocolate onto a marble slab, making a ¼-inch-thick layer. Let cool slightly, but do not let chocolate harden completely.

Using a spatula with a straight metal edge, scrape across chocolate, lifting curls as they form. Refrigerate curls in an airtight container until ready to serve.

Chocolate Designs

Draw or trace on parchment paper designs of your choice. Size of designs should correlate with item on which they are to be used. To make designs, fill a pastry bag with melted

chocolate. Using the fine-line writing tip, outline design in chocolate, following the

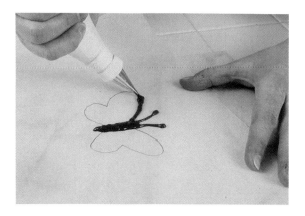

drawn shape. Let design cool in refrigerator. Carefully lift design from paper and store in container until ready to use.

Cantaloupe Flower

Choose a blemish-free cantaloupe. Remove approximately ½ to ¾ inch from the bottom of the melon to form a base. Following the vertical lines of the cantaloupe skin, score the rind in five or more equal sections using a paring knife. (The sections will form petals.) With the paring knife, gently and carefully peel the rind away from the meat of the cantaloupe. Peel the rind sections to within one inch of the bottom.

One third of the way up from the bottom, score the cantaloupe meat into even scallops. Above scallops, using a paring knife, uniformly cut away ⅛ to ¼ inch of cantaloupe meat—this creates the bottom row of scallops. Repeat this process to complete the second row.

For the final row, repeat this process. A shell with a scalloped edge will remain.

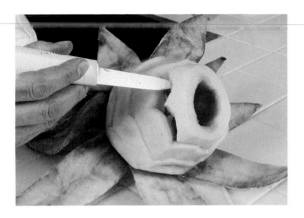

Remove the seeds, scooping from the top of the melon. Fill the shell with your favorite dip or fruit. Make this garnish one day ahead. Use a rubber band to keep the petals folded around the cantaloupe until ready to serve.

Carrot Flowers

Peel a large carrot; remove stem end. Place pointed end on a cutting board. Using a par-

ing knife, turning carrot, make three cuts angled toward the center of the pointed end, creating a three-sided point. To make flowers, hold the carrot with point in one hand and paring knife in the other hand. Move blade up 1 inch from point. Make 3 cuts ⅛ inch thick, parallel to the first cuts, being careful not to slice all the way to the center. Just before reaching the center, curve the knife inward. Carefully remove flower; soak in ice water. Place a stuffed olive or pearl onion in the center of each flower if desired. Note: If the point of the carrot breaks, make another three-sided point and proceed.

Celery Flower

Slice a 2-inch section from the root end of a large bunch of celery. Working on the out-

ermost stalks, use a paring knife to cut scallops to form petals. Continue cutting until all petals are done. Separate the petals slightly. Soak in ice water to open. Trim the root end to make a flat base.

[197]

Scallion Flower

Cut a 3-inch section from the root end of a scallion. Remove the roots but leave the sec-

tion just above them intact. Slice the scallion into many thin slivers being careful not to cut through the end. Immerse in ice water.

Tomato Flower

Using a firm, blemish-free tomato, cherry size or larger, working from the blossom end,

score the skin into five or six equal sections. Gently peel the skin away from the flesh three-fourths of the way down. Carefully peel the petals back; remove the pulp, leaving a shell one-half inch thick. When ready to serve, carefully bend the petals back. Stuff with your favorite salad or dip, or, using a pastry bag, fill with shrimp paste.

Marzipan Pumpkins

Knead 3½ ounces almond paste with 1 to 2 tablespoons confectioners' sugar. For pumpkins, divide dough into small one-inch balls; shape into pumpkins. Using a pastry brush,

lightly coat with orange food coloring. Place a whole clove on top of each pumpkin for a stem. Allow to air dry. Dough can also be tinted and rolled out or shaped into miniature fruits, flowers or animals.

Acorn Squash Rose

Slice the top from the squash; remove seeds, leaving the skin intact. Have the squash sliced paper-thin at a delicatessen. Gently twist a stack of 3 to 5 slices together

to form a small rose. Fasten with a toothpick. The size of each rose depends on the number of slices used.

Tomato Rose

Using a sharp paring knife, begin at the stem end of the tomato and peel the skin away in a ½- to ¾-inch-wide continuous strip. Lemons, oranges or grapefruits can also be used. With citrus fruits, remove as much

of the membrane as possible—the thinner the strip, the better.

To form a rose, roll the strip into a coil ending with the stem end. Fasten with a toothpick. Roses can be made any size desired.

Onion Mum

Select a white or red onion 1 to 2 inches in diameter or larger. The onion should have a single growth. Cut away the top, leaving the root end intact. Using a small paring knife,

make cuts more than halfway into the onion toward the root end. Space the cuts every ¼ inch around the onion. Do not cut through to the root. Immerse in 2 cups hot water with 2 tablespoons of lemon juice to remove odor. Soak in ice water to open the petals.

Radish, Turnip or Beet Mum

Cut off the root and stem ends of the radish. With a sharp paring knife, make vertical cuts almost to the stem end. Make a second row of vertical cuts perpendicular to the

first. Soak in ice water to open the petals. Beets or turnips can also be used; they should be peeled. (Root vegetables are easier to work with at room temperature.)

Vicki T. Chambers of the Floyd S. Kay Vocational Center in Lexington, Virginia, provided her knowledge, enthusiasm and encouragement for this section of *Charleston Entertains*. As a teacher, she has inspired and motivated many students to win culinary awards in various competitions at the state level.

Index

Author Biographies

ANN COPENHAVER COTTON graduated from St. Mary's College, Raleigh, North Carolina, and Salem College, Winston-Salem, North Carolina, with a major in English and a minor in elementary education. Ann was one of the editors of *The Enlightened Gourmet*, a cookbook with nutritional information. Currently, she is teaching kindergarten and is enrolled in the masters of librarianship program at the University of South Carolina. She resides in Charleston with her husband, Phil, and two sons, Jay and Ben.

HENRIETTA FREEMAN GAILLARD graduated from St. Mary's Junior College in Raleigh, North Carolina, and the University of South Carolina in Columbia. Henrietta was one of the editors of *The Enlightened Gourmet*. She lives in Charleston with her husband, Palmer, and two children, Emmie and John, and is currently director of development for Ashley Hall. She is past president of the Junior League of Charleston.

JO ANNE JOYNER WILLIS, R.D., graduated from James Madison University in Harrisonburg, Virginia, and did her dietetic internship at Duke University Medical Center in Durham, North Carolina. Jo Anne was one of the editors of *The Enlightened Gourmet*. She lives in Chattanooga, Tennessee, with her husband, Eddie, and two children, Anne Elliott and Harrison, and currently works as a nutritional consultant.

N. JANE ISELEY lives on a family farm north of Burlington, North Carolina. Jane attended Coker College, and graduated from Radford College with a B.S. degree; she then graduated from the New York Institute of Photography. As staff photographer for Colonial Williamsburg for nine years, she was the photographic author of four books, including *Gardens of Williamsburg*. As a free-lance photographer, Jane has twelve more books to her credit, and is president of Legacy Publications.

Born on the Eastern Shore of Virginia, J. THOMAS SAVAGE, JR., attended St. Andrew's School, Middletown, Delaware, and received a B.A. degree in art history from the College of William and Mary, Williamsburg, Virginia. He holds an M.A. degree in history museum studies from the Cooperstown Graduate Program of the State University of New York. In 1981, Tom was hired as the first full-time curator of Historic Charleston Foundation. He lectures frequently in this country and in England on Charleston architecture and decorative arts.

ALICE TURNER "BOOTS" MICHALAK attended Goucher College and earned a Landscape Design Critics certificate from the University of Maryland. She lives in Arnold, Maryland, with her husband, Andrew, and is the mother of five grown children: Spencer, Liz, Susie, Andrew and John. She is past president of the Annapolis Junior League and has served on the Maryland Governor's Mansion Decorating Committee and the Historic Annapolis Foundation Special Events Committee, and is Chairman of the Christmas Decorating Committee for Historic Annapolis. She lectures and demonstrates flower arranging.